MEDIEVAL CITIES:
THEIR ORIGINS AND THE
REVIVAL OF TRADE

Medieval Cities

THEIR ORIGINS AND THE
REVIVAL OF TRADE

BY HENRI PIRENNE

TRANSLATED FROM THE FRENCH
BY FRANK D. HALSEY

PRINCETON, NEW JERSEY
PRINCETON UNIVERSITY PRESS

19870

TO PRINCETON UNIVERSITY

PREFACE

THIS little volume contains the substance of lectures which I delivered from October to December 1922 in several American universities. It is an attempt to expound, in a general way, the economic awakening and the birth of urban civilization in Western Europe during the Middle Ages.

The bibliography placed at the end of the volume will permit the reader, who may be interested in the subject discussed herein, to inform himself more fully of the details and to verify my assertions. It would be obviously impossible, in a general outline such as this, to go into particulars or take up exceptions and anomalies, and still more so to engage in controversy. Here, then, will be found only a synthesis, the result of long years of study and research.

It is particularly gratifying to me to see this book published by the Press of a University which showed me so cordial a sympathy during the war, and to which I am very happy to dedicate the work as a mark of my profound gratitude.

H. P.

CONTENTS

TRANSLATOR'S FOREWORD

MEDIEVAL CITIES, by Henri Pirenne, was first issued in its English text in 1925 and it was not until two years later, curiously enough, that the book was published (in Brussels) in the language in which it had been written. The English version was reprinted in 1934, and the continuing interest in this stimulating book has now made a new and slightly revised printing advisable.

The occasion has therefore led the translator to reread, for the first time in nearly fifteen years, the original French text. He has as a result been impressed afresh with the author's clarity of thought and facility of expression, but at the same time he has been appalled by the number of infelicities of translation, at least one of which rendered utterly unintelligible the author's meaning. It is to be hoped that the most obvious among them have been corrected in this present printing.

If *Medieval Cities* is not the most important of the author's works—for more than four decades he was a productive scholar—it is one of the most interesting. It is not only a concise "synthesis . . .

of long years of study and research" by one of
the greatest authorities in the field of medieval
history, but is also a noteworthy example of the
best sort of contribution to historical writing, combining simplicity with erudition and imagination
with accuracy. And *Medieval Cities* is possibly of
even more value today than when first published.
In its clear account of the part played by the middle class in the development of the modern economic system and modern culture, it makes us
realize how much cities of the present have borrowed and are borrowing from medieval municipal institutions. It also makes us realize a fact
which had been forgotten, until the rise to power
of the Nazis in Germany and the Fascists in Italy
demonstrated it anew—the importance of the middle class as a revolutionary force. In present-day
Germany and Italy the members of the middle
class, like the inhabitants of the medieval cities
whose economic and in some cases whose actual
physical descendants they are—those "masterless
men" who were neither serfs nor seigneurs—hold
the key to power.

F. D. H.

MEDIEVAL CITIES

Chapter I

THE MEDITERRANEAN

THE Roman Empire, at the end of the third century, had one outstanding general characteristic: it was an essentially Mediterranean commonwealth. Virtually all of its territory lay within the watershed of that great land-locked sea; the distant frontiers of the Rhine, the Danube, the Euphrates and the Sahara, may be regarded merely as an advanced circle of outer defenses protecting the approaches.

The Mediterranean was, without question, the bulwark of both its political and economic unity. Its very existence depended on mastery of the sea. Without that great trade route, neither the government, nor the defense, nor the administration of the *orbis romanus* would have been possible.

As the Empire grew old this fundamentally maritime character was, interestingly enough, not only preserved but was still more sharply defined. When the former inland capital, Rome, was abandoned, its place was taken by a city which not only

served as a capital but which was at the same time
an admirable seaport—Constantinople.

The Empire's cultural development, to be sure,
had clearly passed its peak. Population decreased,
the spirit of enterprise waned, barbarian hordes
commenced to threaten the frontiers, and the increasing expenses of the government, fighting for
its very life, brought in their train a fiscal system
which more and more enslaved men to the State.
Nevertheless this general deterioration does not
seem to have appreciably affected the maritime
commerce of the Mediterranean. It continued to be
active and well sustained, in marked contrast with
the growing apathy that characterized the inland
provinces. Trade continued to keep the East and
the West in close contact with each other. There
was no interruption to the intimate commercial
relations between those diverse climes bathed by
one and the same sea. Both manufactured and
natural products were still extensively dealt in:
textiles from Constantinople, Edessa, Antioch,
and Alexandria; wines, oils and spices from
Syria; papyrus from Egypt; wheat from Egypt,
Africa, and Spain; and wines from Gaul and
Italy. There was even a reform of the monetary
system based on the gold *solidus,* which served
materially to encourage commercial operations by
giving them the benefit of an excellent currency,

universally adopted as an instrument of exchange and as a means of quoting prices.

Of the two great regions of the Empire, the East and the West, the first far surpassed the second, both in superiority of civilization and in a much higher level of economic development. At the beginning of the fourth century there were no longer any really great cities save in the East. The center of the export trade was in Syria and in Asia Minor, and here also was concentrated, in particular, the textile industry for which the whole Roman world was the market and for which Syrian ships were the carriers.

The commercial prominence of the Syrians is one of the most interesting facts in the history of the Lower Empire. It undoubtedly contributed largely to that progressive orientalization of society which was due eventually to end in Byzantinism. And this orientalization, of which the sea was the vehicle, is clear proof of the increasing importance which the Mediterranean acquired as the aging Empire grew weak, gave way in the North beneath the pressure of the barbarians, and contracted more and more about the shores of this inland sea.

The persistence of the Germanic tribes in striving, from the very beginning of the period of the invasions, to reach these same shores and to settle there is worth special notice. When, in the course of the fourth century, the frontiers gave way for the first time under their blows, they poured southward in a living flood. The Quadi and the Marcomanni invaded Italy; the Goths marched on the Bosphorus; the Franks, the Suevi, and the Vandals, who by now had crossed the Rhine, pushed on unhesitatingly towards Aquitaine and Spain. They had no thought of merely colonizing the provinces they coveted. Their dream was rather to settle down, themselves, in those happy regions where the mildness of the climate and the fertility of the soil were matched by the charms and the wealth of civilization.

This initial attempt produced nothing more permanent than the devastation which it had caused. Rome was still strong enough to drive the invaders back beyond the Rhine and the Danube. For a century and a half she succeeded in restraining them, but at the cost of exhausting her armies and her finances.

More and more unequal became the balance of power. The incursions of the barbarians grew more relentless as their increasing numbers made the acquisition of new territory more imperative, while the decreasing population of the Empire made a successful resistance constantly less possible. Despite the extraordinary skill and determination with which the Empire sought to stave off disaster, the outcome was inevitable.

At the beginning of the fifth century, all was over. The whole West was invaded. Roman provinces were transformed into Germanic kingdoms. The Vandals were installed in Africa, the Visigoths in Aquitaine and in Spain, the Burgundians in the Valley of the Rhône, the Ostrogoths in Italy.

This nomenclature is significant. It includes only Mediterranean countries, and little more is needed to show that the objective of the conquerors, free at last to settle down where they pleased, was the sea—that sea which for so long a time the Romans had called, with as much affection as pride, *mare nostrum*. Towards the sea, as of one accord, they all turned their steps, impatient to settle along its shores and to enjoy its beauty.

If the Franks did not reach the Mediterranean at their first attempt, it is because, having come too late, they found the ground already occupied. But they too persisted in striving for a foothold there. One of Clovis's earliest ambitions was to conquer Provence, and only the intervention of Theodoric kept him from extending the frontiers of his kingdom as far as the Côte d'Azur. Yet this first lack of success was not due to discourage his successors. A quarter of a century later, in 536, the Franks made good use of Justinian's offensive against the Ostrogoths and wrung from their hard-pressed rivals the grant of the coveted territory. It is interesting to see how consistently the Merovingian dynasty tended, from that date on, to become in its turn a Mediterranean power.

Childebert and Clotaire, for example, ventured upon an expedition beyond the Pyrenees in 542, which, however, proved to be ill-starred. But it was Italy in particular that aroused the cupidity of the Frankish kings. They formed an alliance, first with the Byzantines and then with the Lombards, in the hope of setting foot south of the Alps. Repeatedly thwarted, they persisted in fresh attempts. By 539, Theudebert had crossed the Alps, and the territories which he had occupied were reconquered by Narses in 553. Numerous efforts were made in 584-585 and from 588 to 590 to get possession anew.

The appearance of the Germanic tribes on the shore of the Mediterranean was by no means a critical point marking the advent of a new era in the history of Europe. Great as were the consequences which it entailed, it did not sweep the boards clean nor even break the tradition. The aim of the invaders was not to destroy the Roman Empire but to occupy and enjoy it. By and large, what they preserved far exceeded what they destroyed or what they brought that was new. It is true that the kingdoms they established on the soil of the Empire made an end of the latter in so far as being a *State* in Western Europe. From a political point of view the *orbis romanus,* now strictly localized in the East, lost that ecumenical character which had made its frontiers coincide with the frontiers of Christianity. The Empire, however, was far from becoming a stranger to the lost provinces. Its civilization there outlived its authority. By the Church, by language, by the superiority of its institutions and law, it prevailed over the conquerors. In the midst of the troubles, the insecurity, the misery and the anarchy which accompanied the invasions there was naturally a certain decline, but even in that decline there was preserved a physiognomy still distinctly Roman. The Germanic tribes were unable, and in fact did not want, to do without it. They barbarized it, but they did not consciously germanize it.

Nothing is better proof of this assertion than the persistence in the last days of the Empire—from the fifth to the eighth century—of that maritime character pointed out above. The importance of the Mediterranean did not grow less after the period of the invasions. The sea remained for the Germanic tribes what it had been before their arrival—the very center of Europe, the *mare nostrum.* The sea had had such great importance in the political order that the deposing of the last Roman Emperor in the West (476) was not enough in itself to turn historical evolution from its time-honored direction. It continued, on the contrary, to develop in the same theater and under the same influences. No indication yet gave warning of the end of that commonwealth of civilization created by the Empire from the Pillars of Hercules to the Aegean Sea, from the coasts of Egypt and Africa to the shores of Gaul, Italy and Spain. In spite of the invasion of the barbarians the new world conserved, in all essential characteristics, the physiognomy of the old. To follow the course of events from Romulus Augustulus to Charlemagne it is necessary to keep the Mediterranean constantly in view.

All the great events in political history are unfolded on its shores. From 493 to 526 Italy, governed by Theodoric, maintained a hegemony over all the Germanic kingdoms, a hegemony through which the power of the Roman tradition was perpetuated and assured. After Theodoric, this power was still more clearly shown. Justinian failed by but little of restoring imperial unity (527-565). Africa, Spain, and Italy were reconquered. The Mediterranean became again a Roman lake. Byzantium, it is true, weakened by the immense effort she had just put forth, could neither finish nor even preserve intact the astonishing work which she had accomplished. The Lombards took Northern Italy away from her (568); the Visigoths freed themselves from her yoke. Nevertheless she did not abandon her ambitions. She retained, for a long time to come, Africa, Sicily, Southern Italy. Nor did she loose her grip on the West—thanks to the sea, the mastery of which her fleets so securely held that the fate of Europe rested at that moment, more than ever, on the waves of the Mediterranean.

What was true of the political situation held equally well for the cultural. It seems hardly necessary to recall that Boëthius (480-525) and Cassiodorus (477-c.562) were Italians as were St. Benedict (480-534) and Gregory the Great (590-604), and that Isidorus of Seville (570-636) was a Spaniard. It was Italy that maintained the last schools at the same time that she was fostering the spread of monachism north of the Alps. It was in Italy, also, that what was left of the ancient culture flourished side by side with what was brought forth anew in the bosom of the Church. All the strength and vigor that the Church possessed was concentrated in the region of the Mediterranean. There alone she gave evidence of an organization and spirit capable of initiating great enterprises.

An interesting example of this is the fact that
Christianity was brought to the Anglo-Saxons
(596) from the distant shores of Italy, not from
the neighboring shores of Gaul. The mission of St.
Augustine is therefore an illuminating sidelight
on the historic influence retained by the Mediterranean. And it seems more significant still when
we recall that the evangelization of Ireland was
due to missionaries sent out from Marseilles, and
that the apostles of Belgium, St. Amand (689-
693) and St. Remade (*c.* 668), were Aquitanians.

A brief survey of the economic development of
Europe will give the crowning touch to the sub-
stantiation of the theory which has here been put
forward. That development is, obviously, a clear-
cut, direct continuation of the economy of the
Roman Empire. In it are rediscovered all the latter's principal traits and, above all, that Mediterranean character which here is unmistakable. To
be sure, a general decline in social activity was
apparent in this region as in all others. By the last
days of the Empire there was a clearly marked decline which the catastrophe of the invasions naturally helped accentuate. But it would be a decided
mistake to imagine that the arrival of the Germanic tribes had as a result the substitution of a
purely agricultural economy and a general stag-

nation in trade for urban life and commercial
activity.[1]

The supposed dislike of the barbarians for
towns is an admitted fable to which reality has
given the lie. If, on the extreme frontiers of the
Empire, certain towns were put to the torch, destroyed and pillaged, it is none the less true that
the immense majority survived the invasions. A
statistical survey of cities in existence at the present day in France, in Italy and even on the banks
of the Rhine and the Danube, gives proof that,
for the most part, these cities now stand on the
sites where rose the Roman cities, and that their
very names are often but a transformation of
Roman names.

The Church had of course closely patterned the
religious districts after the administrative districts
of the Empire. As a general rule, each diocese corresponded to a *civitas*. Since the ecclesiastical organization suffered no change during the era of
the Germanic invasions, the result was that in the
new kingdoms founded by the conquerors it preserved intact this characteristic feature. In fact,
from the beginning of the sixth century the word
civitas took the special meaning of "episcopal

[1] A. Dopsch, *Wirtschaftliche und soziale Grundlagen der euro-
päischen Kulturentwicklung*, Vienna, 1920, Vol. II, p. 527, takes
issue strongly with the opinion that the Germanic invasions put
an end to Roman civilization.

city," the center of the diocese. In surviving the
Empire on which it was based, the Church therefore contributed very largely to the safeguarding
of the existence of the Roman cities.

But it must not be overlooked, on the other
hand, that these cities in themselves long retained
a considerable importance. Their municipal institutions did not suddenly disappear upon the
arrival of the Germanic tribes. Not only in Italy,
but also in Spain and even in Gaul, they kept
their *decuriones*—a corps of magistrates provided with a judicial and administrative authority, the details of which are not clear but whose
existence and Roman origin is a matter of record.
There is to be noticed, moreover, the presence of
the *defensor civitatis,* and the practice of inscrib-
ing notarized deeds in the *gesta municipalia.*

It is also well established that these cities were
the centers of an economic activity which itself
was a survival of the preceding civilization. Each
city was the market for the surrounding countryside, the winter home of the great landed proprietors of the neighborhood and, if favorably situated, the center of a commerce the more highly developed in proportion to its nearness to the shores
of the Mediterranean. A perusal of Gregory of
Tours gives ample proof that in the Gaul of his
time there was still a professional merchant class

residing in the towns. He cites, in some thoroughly characteristic passages, those of Verdun, Paris, Orleans, Clermont-Ferrand, Marseilles, Nimes, and Bordeaux, and the information which he supplies concerning them is all the more significant in that it is brought into his narrative only incidentally. Care should of course be taken not to exaggerate its value. An equally great fault would be to undervalue it. Certainly the economic order of Merovingian Gaul was founded on agriculture rather than on any other form of activity. More certainly still this had already been the case under the Roman Empire.

But this does not preclude the fact that inland traffic, the import and export of goods and merchandise, was carried on to a considerable extent. It was an important factor in the maintenance of society. An indirect proof of this is furnished by the institution of market-tolls (*teloneum*). Thus were called the tolls set up by the Roman administration along the roads, in the ports, at bridges and fords, and elsewhere. The Frankish kings let them all stay in force and drew from them such copious revenues that the collectors of this class of taxes (*telonearii*) figured among their most useful functionaries.

The continued commercial activity after the disappearance of the Empire, and, likewise, the survival of the towns that were the centers thereof and the merchants who were its instruments, is explained by the continuation of Mediterranean trade. In all the chief characteristics it was the same, from the fifth to the eighth centuries, as it had been just after Constantine. If, as is probable, the decline was the more rapid after the Germanic invasions, it remains none the less true that there is presented a picture of uninterrupted intercourse between the Byzantine East and the West dominated by the barbarians. By means of the shipping which was carried on from the coasts of Spain and Gaul to those of Syria and Asia Minor, the basin of the Mediterranean did not cease, despite the political subdivisions which it had seen take place, to consolidate the economic unity which it had shaped for centuries under the imperial commonwealth. Because of this fact, the economic organization of the world lived on after the political transformation.

In lack of other proofs, the monetary system of the Frankish kings would alone establish this truth convincingly. This system, as is too well known to make necessary any lengthy consideration here, was purely Roman or, strictly speaking, Romano-Byzantine. This is shown by the coins that were minted: the *solidus,* the *triens,* and the *denarius*—that is to say, the *sou,* the *third-*

sou and the *denier*. It is shown further by the
metal which was employed: gold, used for the
coinage of the *solidus* and the *triens*. It is also
shown by the weight which was given to specie. It
is shown, finally, by the effigies which were minted
on the coins. In this connection it is worth noting
that the mints continued for a long time, under
the Merovingian kings, the custom of representing
the bust of the Emperor on the coins and of showing on the reverse of the pieces the *Victoria
Augusti* and that, carrying this imitation to the
extreme, when the Byzantines substituted the cross
for the symbol of that victory they did the same.
Such extreme servility can be explained only by
the continuing influence of the Empire. The obvious reason was the necessity of preserving, between the local currency and the imperial currency, a conformity which would be purposeless
if the most intimate relations had not existed between Merovingian commerce and the general
commerce of the Mediterranean. In other words,
this commerce continued to be closely bound up
with the commerce of the Byzantine Empire. Of
such ties, moreover, there are abundant proofs
and it will suffice to mention merely a few of the
most significant.

It should be borne in mind, first of all, that at
the start of the eighth century Marseilles was

still the great port of Gaul. The terms employed
by Gregory of Tours, in the numerous anecdotes
in which he happens to speak of that city, make
it seem a singularly animated economic center. A
very active shipping bound it to Constantinople,
to Syria, Africa, Egypt, Spain and Italy. The
products of the East—papyrus, spices, costly textiles, wine and oil—were the basis of a regular import trade. Foreign merchants, Jews and Syrians
for the most part, had their residence there, and
their nationality is itself an indication of the close
relations kept up by Marseilles with Byzantium.
Finally, the extraordinary quantity of coins which
were struck there during the Merovingian era
gives material proof of the activity of its commerce. The population of the city must have
comprised, aside from the merchants, a rather
numerous class of artisans.[2] In every respect it
seems, then, to have accurately preserved, under
the government of the Frankish kings, the clearly
municipal character of Roman cities.

The economic development of Marseilles naturally made itself felt in the hinterland of the port.
Under its attraction, all the commerce of Gaul
was oriented toward the Mediterranean. The most

[2] It is impossible, in fact, not to infer that at Marseilles there
was a class of artisans at least as important as that which still
existed at Arles in the middle of the sixth century. See F. Kiener,
Verfassungsgeschichte der Provence, Leipzig, 1900, p. 29.

important market-tolls of the Frankish kingdom
were situated in the neighborhood of the town at
Fos, at Arles, at Toulon, at Sorgues, at Valence,
at Vienne, and at Avignon. Here is clear proof
that merchandise landed in the city was expedited
to the interior. By the course of the Rhône and of
the Saone, as well as by the Roman roads, it
reached the north of the country. The charters are
still in existence by which the Abbey of Corbie
(Department of Pas-de-Calais) obtained from
the kings an exemption from tolls at Fos on a
number of commodities, among which may be re-
marked a surprising variety of spices of eastern
origin, as well as papyrus. In these circumstances
it does not seem unwarranted to assume that the
commercial activity of the ports of Rouen and
Nantes, on the shores of the Atlantic Ocean, as
well as of Quentovic and Duurstede, on the shores
of the North Sea, was sustained by the ramifica-
tions of the export traffic from far-off Marseilles.

But it was in the south of the country that this
effect was the most appreciable. All the largest
cities of Merovingian Gaul were still to be found,
as in the days of the Roman Empire, south of the
Loire. The details which Gregory of Tours supplies concerning Clermont-Ferrand and Orleans
show that they had within their walls veritable
colonies of Jews and Syrians, and if it was so with

those towns which there is no reason for believing enjoyed a privileged status, it must have been so also with the much more important centers such as Bordeaux or Lyons. It is an established fact, moreover, that Lyons still had at the Carolingian era a quite numerous Jewish population.

Here, then, is quite enough to support the conclusion that Merovingian times knew, thanks to the continuance of Mediterranean shipping and the intermediary of Marseilles, what we may safely call a great commerce. It would certainly be an error to assume that the dealings of the oriental merchants of Gaul were restricted solely to articles of luxury. Probably the sale of jewelry, enamels and silk stuffs resulted in handsome profits, but this would not be enough to explain their number and their extraordinary diffusion throughout all the country. The traffic of Marseilles was, above all else, supported by goods for general consumption such as wine and oil, spices and papyrus. These commodities, as has already been pointed out, were regularly exported to the north.

The oriental merchants of the Frankish Empire were virtually engaged in wholesale trade. Their boats, after being discharged on the quays of Marseilles, certainly carried back, on leaving the shores of Provence, not only passengers but return freight. Our sources of information, to be sure, do not tell much about the nature of this freight. Among the possible conjectures, one of the most likely is that it probably consisted, at least in good part, in human chattels—that is to say, in slaves. Traffic in slaves did not cease to be carried on in the Frankish Empire until the end of the ninth century. The wars waged against the barbarians of Saxony, Thuringia and the Slavic regions provided a source of supply which seems to have been abundant enough. Gregory of Tours speaks of Saxon slaves belonging to a merchant of Orleans, and it is a good guess that this Samo, who departed in the first half of the seventh century with a band of companions for the country of Wends, whose king he eventually became, was very probably nothing more than an adventurer trafficking in slaves. And it is of course obvious that the slave trade, to which the Jews still assiduously applied themselves in the ninth century, must have had its origin in an earlier era.

If the bulk of the commerce in Merovingian Gaul was to be found in the hands of oriental merchants, their influence, however, should not be exaggerated. Side by side with them. and according to all indications in constant relations with them, are mentioned indigenous merchants. Gregory of Tours does not fail to supply information concerning them, which would undoubtedly have been more voluminous if his narrative had had more than a merely incidental interest in them. He shows the king consenting to a loan to the merchants of Verdun, whose business prospers so well that they soon find themselves in a position to reimburse him. He mentions the existence in Paris of a *domus negociantum*—that is to say, apparently, of a sort of market or bazaar. He speaks of a merchant profiteering during the great famine of 585 and getting rich. And in all these anecdotes he is dealing, without the least doubt, with professionals and not with merely casual buyers or sellers.

The picture which the commerce of Merovingian Gaul presents is repeated, naturally, in the other maritime Germanic kingdoms of the Mediterranean—among the Ostrogoths of Italy, among the Vandals of Africa, among the Visigoths of Spain. The Edict of Theodoric contained a quantity of stipulations relative to merchants. Carthage continued to be an important port in close relations with Spain, and her ships, apparently, went up the coast as far as Bordeaux. The laws of the Visigoths mentioned merchants from overseas.

In all of this is clearly manifest the vigorous continuity of the commercial development of the Roman Empire after the Germanic invasions. They did not put an end to the economic unity of antiquity. By means of the Mediterranean and the relations kept up thereby between the West and the East, this unity, on the contrary, was preserved with a remarkable distinctiveness. The great inland sea of Europe no longer belonged, as before, to a single State. But nothing yet gave reason to predict that it would soon cease to have its time-honored importance. Despite the transformations which it had undergone, the new world had not lost the Mediterranean character of the old. On the shores of the sea was still concentrated the better part of its activities. No indication yet gave warning of the end of the commonwealth of civilization, created by the Roman Empire from the Pillars of Hercules to the Aegean Sea. At the beginning of the seventh century, anyone who sought to look into the future would have been unable to discern any reason for not believing in the continuance of the old tradition.

Yet what was then natural and reasonable to predict was not to be realized. The world-order which had survived the Germanic invasions was not able to survive the invasion of Islam.

It is thrown across the path of history with the elemental force of a cosmic cataclysm. Even in the lifetime of Mahomet (571-632) no one could have imagined the consequences or have prepared for them. Yet the movement took no more than fifty

years to spread from the China Sea to the Atlantic
Ocean. Nothing was able to withstand it. At the
first blow, it overthrew the Persian Empire (637-
644). It took from the Byzantine Empire, in quick
succession, Syria (634-636), Egypt (640-642),
Africa (698). It reached into Spain (711). The
resistless advance was not to slow down until the
start of the eighth century, when the walls of Constantinople on the one side (713) and the soldiers
of Charles Martel on the other (732) broke that
great enveloping offensive against the two flanks
of Christianity.

But if its force of expansion was exhausted, it
had none the less changed the face of the world.
Its sudden thrust had destroyed ancient Europe.
It had put an end to the Mediterranean commonwealth in which it had gathered its strength.

The familiar and almost "family" sea which
once united all the parts of this commonwealth
was to become a barrier between them. On all its
shores, for centuries, social life, in its fundamental characteristics, had been the same; religion, the same; customs and ideas, the same or
very nearly so. The invasion of the barbarians
from the North had modified nothing essential
in that situation.

But now, all of a sudden, the very lands where
civilization had been born were torn away; the

Cult of the Prophet was substituted for the Christian Faith, Moslem law for Roman law, the Arab tongue for the Greek and the Latin tongue.

The Mediterranean had been a Roman lake; it now became, for the most part, a Moslem lake. From this time on it separated, instead of uniting, the East and the West of Europe. The tie which was still binding the Byzantine Empire to the Germanic kingdoms of the West was broken.

Chapter II

The Ninth Century

THE tremendous effect the invasion of Islam had upon Western Europe has not, perhaps, been fully appreciated.

Out of it arose a new and unparalleled situation, unlike anything that had gone before. Through the Phoenicians, the Greeks, and finally the Romans, Western Europe had always received the cultural stamp of the East. It had lived, as it were, by virtue of the Mediterranean; now for the first time it was forced to live by its own resources. The center of gravity, heretofore on the shore of the Mediterranean, was shifted to the north. As a result the Frankish Empire, which had so far been playing only a minor rôle in the history of Europe, was to become the arbiter of Europe's destinies.

There is obviously more than mere coincidence in the simultaneity of the closing of the Mediterranean by Islam and the entry of the Carolingians on the scene. There is the distinct relation of cause and effect between the two. The Frankish Empire

was fated to lay the foundations of the Europe of
the Middle Ages. But the mission which it fulfilled had as an essential prior condition the overthrow of the traditional world-order. The Carolingians would never have been called upon to
play the part they did if historical evolution had
not been turned aside from its course and, so to
speak, "de-Saxoned" by the Moslem invasion.
Without Islam, the Frankish Empire would probably never have existed and Charlemagne, without Mahomet, would be inconceivable.

This is made plain enough by the many contrasts between the Merovingian era, during which
the Mediterranean retained its time-honored historical importance, and the Carolingian era, when
that influence ceased to make itself felt. These
contrasts were in evidence everywhere: in religious sentiment, in political and social institutions,
in literature, in language and even in handwrit-
ing. From whatever standpoint it is studied, the
civilization of the ninth century shows a distinct
break with the civilization of antiquity. Nothing
would be more fallacious than to see therein a
simple continuation of the preceding centuries.
The *coup d'état* of Pepin the Short was considerably more than the substitution of one dynasty for
another. It marked a new orientation of the course
hitherto followed by history. At first glance there

seems reason to believe that Charlemagne, in assuming the title of Roman Emperor and of Augustus, wished to restore the ancient tradition. In reality, in setting himself up against the Emperor of Constantinople, he broke that tradition. His Empire was Roman only in so far as the Catholic Church was Roman. For it was from the Church, and the Church alone, that came its inspiration. The forces which he placed at her service were, moreover, forces of the north. His principal collaborators, in religious and cultural matters, were no longer, as they had previously been, Italians, Aquitanians, or Spaniards; they were Anglo-Saxons—a St. Boniface or an Alcuin—or they were Swabians, like Einhard. In the affairs of the State, which was now cut off from the Mediterranean, southerners played scarcely any rôle. The Germanic influence commenced to dominate at the very moment when the Frankish Empire, forced to turn away from the Mediterranean, spread over Northern Europe and pushed its frontiers as far as the Elbe and the mountains of Bohemia.[1]

[1] The objection may be raised that Charlemagne conquered in Italy the kingdom of the Lombards and in Spain the region included between the Pyrenees and the Ebro. But these thrusts towards the south are by no means to be explained by a desire to dominate the shores of the Mediterranean. The expeditions

In the field of economics the contrast, which the Carolingian period shows to Merovingian times, is especially striking. In the days of the Merovingians, Gaul was still a maritime country and trade and traffic flourished because of that fact. The Empire of Charlemagne, on the contrary, was essentially an inland one. No longer was there any communication with the exterior; it was a closed State, a State without foreign markets, living in a condition of almost complete isolation.

To be sure, the transition from one era to the other was not clear-cut. The trade of Marseilles did not suddenly cease but, from the middle of the seventh century, waned gradually as the Moslems advanced in the Mediterranean. Syria, conquered by them in 633-638, no longer kept it thriving with her ships and her merchandise. Shortly afterwards, Egypt passed in her turn under the yoke of Islam (638-640), and papyrus no longer came to Gaul. A characteristic consequence is that, after 677, the royal chancellery stopped using papyrus.[2]

against the Lombards were provoked by political causes and especially by the alliance with the Papacy. The expedition in Spain had no other aim than the establishing of a solid frontier against the Moslems.

[2] Imports, however, had not completely ceased at that date. The last reference we know to the use of papyrus in Gaul is in 737; see M. Prou, *Manuel de paléographie*, 3rd edit., p. 17. In Italy, it was continued to be used up to the eleventh century; see A. Giry, *Manuel de diplomatique*, p. 494. It was imported there either from Egypt or, more probably, from Sicily (where the Arabs had in-

The importation of spices kept up for a while, for
the monks of Corbie, in 716, believed it useful to
have ratified for the last time their privileges of
the *tonlieu* of Fos. A half century later, solitude
reigned in the port of Marseilles. Her foster-
mother, the sea, was shut off from her and the
economic life of the inland regions which had
been nourished through her intermediary was definitely extinguished. By the ninth century Provence, once the richest country of Gaul, had become the poorest.

More and more, the Moslems consolidated their
domination over the sea. In the course of the ninth
century they seized the Balearic Isles, Corsica,
Sardinia, Sicily. On the coasts of Africa they
founded new ports: Tunis (698-703); later on,
Mehdia to the south of this city; then Cairo, in
973. Palermo, where stood a great arsenal, became their principal base in the Tyrrhenian Sea.
Their fleets sailed it in complete mastery; commercial flotillas transported the products of the
West to Cairo, whence they were redispatched to
Bagdad, or pirate fleets devastated the coasts of
Provence and Italy and put towns to the torch
after they had been pillaged and their inhabitants

troduced its manufacture) by the shipping of the Byzantine cities
of the South of the Peninsula, or by that of Venice, which will
be discussed in Chap. III.

captured to be sold as slaves. In 889 a band of
these plunderers even laid hold of Fraxinetum
(the present Garde-Frainet, in the Department of
the Var) not far from Nice, the garrison of which,
for nearly a century thereafter, subjected the
neighboring populace to continual raids and men-
aced the roads which led across the Alps from
France to Italy.

The efforts of Charlemagne and his successors
to protect the coasts from Saracen raiders were as
impotent as their attempts to oppose the invasions
of the Norsemen in the north and west. The
hardihood and seamanship of the Danes and Norwegians made it easy for them to plunder the
coasts of the Carolingian Empire during the whole
of the eleventh century. They conducted their
raids not only from the North Sea, the Channel,
and the Gulf of Gascony, but at times even from
the Mediterranean. Every river which emptied
into these seas was, at one time or another, as-
cended by their skilfully constructed barks, splendid specimens whereof, brought to light by recent
excavations, are now preserved at Oslo. Periodically the valleys of the Rhine, the Meuse, the
Scheldt, the Seine, the Loire, the Garonne and the
Rhône were the scene of systematic and persistent
pillaging. The devastation was so complete that,
in many cases indeed, the population itself disap-

peared. And nothing is a better illustration of the essentially inland character of the Frankish Empire than its inability to organize the defense of its coasts, against either Saracens or Norsemen. For that defense, to be effective, should have been a naval defense, and the Empire had no fleets, or hastily improvised ones at best.

Such conditions were incompatible with the existence of a commerce of first-rate importance. The historical literature of the ninth century contains, it is true, certain references to merchants (*mercatores, negociatores*),[3] but no illusion should be cherished as to their importance. Compared to the number of texts which have been preserved from that era, these references are extremely rare. The capitularies, those regulations touching upon every phase of social life, are remarkably meagre in so far as applies to commerce. From this it may be assumed that the latter played a rôle of only secondary, negligible importance. It was only in the north of Gaul that, during the first half of

[3] A. Dopsch, *Die Wirtschaftsentwicklung der Karolingerzeit*, Vol. II, pp. 180 *ff.*, has, with very great erudition, cited a number of them. We must, however, bear in mind that many among them belong to the Merovingian period and that many others are far from having the significance which he attributes to them. See also J. W. Thompson, "The Commerce of France in the Ninth Century," *The Journal of Political Economy*, 1915, Vol. XXIII, p. 857.

the ninth century, trade showed any signs of activity.

The ports of Quentovic (a place now vanished, near Etaples in the Department of Pas-de-Calais) and Duurstede (on the Rhine, southwest of Utrecht) which under the Merovingian monarchy were already trading with England and Denmark, seem to have been centers of a widely extended shipping. It is a safe conjecture that because of them the river transport of the Friesians along the Rhine, the Scheldt and the Meuse enjoyed an importance that was matched by no other region during the reigns of Charlemagne and his successors. The cloths woven by the peasants of Flanders, and which contemporary texts designate by the name of Friesian cloaks (*pallia fresonica*), together with the wines of Rhenish Germany, supplied to that river traffic the substance of an export trade which seems to have been fairly regular up to the day when the Norsemen took possession of the ports in question. It is known, moreover, that the *deniers* coined at Duurstede had a very extensive circulation. They served as prototypes for the oldest coins of Sweden and Poland, evident proof that they early penetrated, no doubt at the hands of the Norsemen, as far as the Baltic Sea. Attention may also be called, as having been the substance of a rather extensive trade, to the salt industry of Noirmoutier, where Irish ships were to be seen. Salzburg salt, on the other hand, was shipped along the Danube and its affluents to the interior of the Empire. The sale of slaves, despite the prohibitions that were laid down by the sovereigns, was carried on along the western frontiers, where the prisoners of war taken from among the pagan Slavs found numerous purchasers.

The Jews seem to have applied themselves particularly to this sort of traffic. They were still numerous, and were found in every part of Francia. Those in the south of Gaul were in close relations with their coreligionists of Moslem Spain, to whom they are accused of having sold Christian children.

It was probably from Spain, or perhaps also from Venice, that these Jews obtained the spices and the valuable textiles in which they dealt. However, the obligation to which they were subjected of having their children baptized must have caused a great number of them to emigrate south of the Pyrenees at an early date, and their commercial importance steadily declined in the course of the ninth century. As for the Syrians, they were no longer of importance at this era.[4]

[4] The ingenious attempt of Mr. J. W. Thompson to prove the contrary, in his work cited in note 3 above, raises philological

It is, then, most likely that the commerce of Carolingian times was very much reduced. Except in the neighborhood of Quentovic and Duurstede, it consisted only in the transport of indispensable commodities, such as wine and salt, in the prohibited traffic of a few slaves, and in the barter, through the intermediary of the Jews, of a small number of products from the East.

Of a regular and normal commercial activity, of steady trading carried on by a class of professional merchants, in short, of all that constitutes the very essence of an economy of exchange worthy of the name, no traces are to be found after the closing off of the Mediterranean by the Islamic invasion. The great number of markets (*mercatus*), which were to be found in the ninth century, in no way contradicts this assertion. They were, as a matter of fact, only small local marketplaces, instituted for the weekly provisioning of the populace by means of the retail sale of foodstuffs from the country. As a proof of the commercial activity of the Carolingian era, it would be equally beside the point to speak of the existence of the street occupied by merchants (*vicus mercatorum*) at Aix-la-Chapelle near the palace of Charlemagne, or of similar streets near certain

difficulties which prevent our adopting it. The Greek origin of the work *Cappi*, upon which it is based, cannot be accepted.

great abbeys such as, for example, that of St.
Riquier. The merchants with whom we have to
do here were not, in fact, professional merchants
but servitors charged with the duty of supplying
the Court or the monks. They were, so to speak,
employees of the seignorial household staff and
were in no respect merchants.

There is, moreover, material proof of the economic decline which affected Western Europe
from the day when she ceased to belong to the
Mediterranean commonwealth. It is furnished by
the reform of the monetary system, initiated by
Pepin the Short and completed by Charlemagne.
That reform abandoned gold coinage and substituted silver in its place. The *solidus* which had
heretofore, conforming to the Roman tradition,
constituted the basic monetary unit, was now only
nominal money. The only real coins from this
time on were the silver *deniers*, weighing about
two grams, the metallic value of which, compared
to that of the dollar, was approximately eight and
one-half cents. The metallic value of the Merovingian gold *solidus* being nearly three dollars, the
importance of the reform can be readily appreciated. Undoubtedly it is to be explained only by
a prodigious falling off of both trading and
wealth.

If it is admitted, and it must be admitted, that
the reappearance of gold coinage, with the florins
of Florence and the ducats of Venice in the thirteenth century, characterized the economic renaissance of Europe, the inverse is also true: the aban-
doning of gold coinage in the eighth century was
the manifestation of a profound decline. It is not
enough to say that Pepin and Charlemagne
wished to remedy the monetary disorder of the
last days of the Merovingian era. It would have
been quite possible for them to find a remedy
without giving up the gold standard. They gave
up the standard, obviously, from necessity—that
is to say, as a result of the disappearance of the
yellow metal in Gaul. And this disappearance had
no other cause than the interruption of the commerce of the Mediterranean. The proof of this is
given by the fact that Southern Italy, remaining
in contact with Constantinople, retained like the
latter a gold standard, for which the Carolingian
sovereigns were forced to substitute a silver standard. The very light weight of their *deniers,*
moreover, testifies to the economic isolation of
their Empire. It is inconceivable that they would
have reduced the monetary unit to a thirtieth of
its former value if there had been preserved the
slightest bond between their States and the Medi-

terranean regions where the gold *solidus* continued to circulate.

But this is not all. The monetary reform of the ninth century not only was in keeping with the general impoverishment of the era in which it took place, but with the circulation of money which was noteworthy for both lightness and inadequacy. In the absence of centers of attraction sufficiently powerful to draw money from afar, it remained, so to speak, stagnant. Charlemagne and his successors in vain ordered that *deniers* should be coined only in the royal mints. Under the reign of Louis the Pious, it was necessary to give to certain churches authorization to coin money, in view of the difficulties, under which they labored, of obtaining cash. From the second half of the ninth century on, the authorization to establish a market was almost always accompanied by the authorization to establish a mint in the same place. The State could not retain the monopoly of minting coins. It was consistently frittered away. And that is again a manifestation, by no means equivocal, of the economic decline. History shows that the better commerce is sustained, the more the monetary system is centralized and simplified. The dispersion, the variety, and in fact the anarchy which it manifests as we follow the course of the ninth century, ends by giving striking confirmation to the general theory here put forward.

There have been some attempts to attribute to Charlemagne a far-seeing political economy. This is to lend him ideas which, however great we suppose his genius to have been, it is impossible for him to have had. No one can submit with any likelihood of truth that the projects which he commenced in 793, to join the Rednitz to the Altmühl and so establish communication between the Rhine and the Danube, could have had any other purpose than the transport of troops, or that the wars against the Avars were provoked by the desire to open up a commercial route to Constantinople. The stipulations, in other respects inoperative, of the capitularies regarding coinages, weights and measures, the market-tolls and the markets, were intimately bound up with the general system of regulation and control which was typical of Carolingian legislation. The same is true regarding the measures taken against usury and the prohibition enjoining members of the clergy from engaging in business. Their purpose was to combat fraud, disorder and indiscipline and to impose a Christian morality on the people. Only a prejudiced point of view can see in them an attempt to stimulate the economic development of the Empire.

We are so accustomed to consider the reign of
Charlemagne as an era of revival that we are un-
consciously led to imagine an identical progress in
all fields. Unfortunately, what is true of literary
culture, of the religious State, of customs, institutions and statecraft is not true of communications and commerce. Every great thing that
Charlemagne accomplished was accomplished
either by his military strength or by his alliance
with the Church. For that matter, neither the
Church nor arms could overcome the circumstances in virtue of which the Frankish Empire
found itself deprived of foreign markets. It was
forced, in fact, to accommodate itself to a situation which was inevitably prescribed. History
is obliged to recognize that, however brilliant it
seems in other respects, the cycle of Charlemagne,
considered from an economic viewpoint, is a cycle
of regression.

The financial organization of the Frankish
Empire makes this plain. It was, indeed, as rudi-
mentary as could be. The poll tax, which the
Merovingians had preserved in imitation of
Rome, no longer existed. The resources of the
sovereign consisted only in the revenue from his
demesnes, in the tributes levied on conquered
tribes and in the booty got by war. The market-
tolls no longer contributed to the replenishment

of the treasury, thus attesting to the commercial decline of the period. They were nothing more than a simple extortion brutally levied in kind on the infrequent merchandise transported by the rivers or along the roads. The sorry proceeds, which should have served to keep up the bridges, the docks and the highways, were swallowed up by the functionaries who collected them. The *missi dominici*, created to supervise their administration, were impotent in abolishing the abuses which they proved to exist because the State, unable to pay its agents, was likewise unable to impose its authority on them. It was obliged to call on the aristocracy which, thanks to their social status, alone could give free services. But in so doing it was constrained, for lack of money, to chose the instruments of power from among the midst of a group of men whose most evident interest was to diminish that power. The recruiting of the functionaries from among the aristocracy was the fundamental vice of the Frankish Empire and the essential cause of its dissolution, which became so rapid after the death of Charlemagne. Surely, nothing is more fragile than that State the sovereign of which, all-powerful in theory, is dependent in fact upon the fidelity of his independent agents.

The feudal system was in embryo in this contradictory situation. The Carolingian Empire would have been able to keep going only if it had possessed, like the Byzantine Empire or the Empire of the Caliphs, a tax system, a financial control, a fiscal centralization and a treasury providing for the salary of functionaries, for public works, and for the maintenance of the army and the navy. The financial impotence which caused its downfall was a clear demonstration of the impossibility it encountered of maintaining a political structure on an economic base which was no longer able to support the load.

That economic base of the State, as of society, was from this time on the landed proprietor. Just as the Carolingian Empire was an inland State without foreign markets, so also was it an essentially agricultural State. The traces of commerce which were still to be found there were negligible. There was no other property than landed property, and no other work than rural work. As has already been stated above, this predominance of agriculture was no new fact. It existed in a very distinct form in the Roman era and it continued with increasing strength in the Merovingian era. As early as the close of antiquity, all the west of Europe was covered with great demesnes belonging to an aristocracy the members of which bore the title of senators (*senatores*). More and more, property was disappearing in a transformation into hereditary tenures, while the old free farmers were themselves undergoing a transformation into "cultivators" (*coloni*) bound to the soil, from father to son. The Germanic invasions did not noticeably alter this state of things. We have definitely given up the idea of picturing the Germanic tribes in the light of a democracy of peasants, all on an equal footing. Social distinctions were very great among them even when they first invaded the Empire. They comprised a minority of the wealthy and a majority of the poor. The number of slaves and half-free (*liti*) was considerable.

The arrival of the invaders in the Roman provinces brought with it, then, no overthrow of the existing order. The newcomers preserved, in adapting themselves thereto, the status quo. Many of the invaders received from the king or acquired by force or by marriage, or otherwise, great demesnes which made them the equals of the "senators." The landed aristocracy, far from disappearing, was on the contrary invigorated by new elements.

The disappearance of the small free proprietors continued. It seems, in fact, that as early as the start of the Carolingian period only a very small number of them still existed in Gaul.

Charlemagne in vain took measures to safeguard those who were left. The need of protection inevitably made them turn to the more powerful individuals to whose patronage they subordinated their persons and their possessions.

Large estates, then, kept on being more and more generally in evidence after the period of the invasions. The favor which the kings showed the Church was an additional factor in this development, and the religious fervor of the aristocracy had the same effect. Monasteries, whose number multiplied with such remarkable rapidity after the seventh century, were receiving bountiful gifts of land. Everywhere ecclesiastical demesnes and lay demesnes were mixed up together, uniting not only cultivated ground, but woods, heaths and waste-lands.

The organization of these demesnes remained in conformity, in Frankish Gaul, with what it had been in Roman Gaul. It is clear that this could not have been otherwise. The Germanic tribes had no motive for, and were, furthermore, incapable of, substituting a different organization. It consisted, in its essentials, of classifying all the land in two groups, subject to two distinct forms of government. The first, the less extensive, was directly exploited by the proprietor; the second was divided, under deeds of tenure, among the peasants. Each of the *villae* of which a demesne was composed comprised both seignorial land (*terra dominicata*) and censal land, divided in units of cultivation (*mansus*) held by hereditary right by manants or villeins (*manentes, villani*) in return for the prestation of rents, in money or in kind, and statute-labor.[5]

As long as urban life and commerce flourished, the great demesnes had a market for the disposal of their produce. There is no room for doubt that during all the Merovingian era it was through them that the city groups were provisioned and that the merchants were supplied. But it could not help be otherwise when trade disappeared and therewith the merchant class and the municipal population. The great estates suffered the same fate as the Frankish Empire. Like it, they lost their markets. The possibility of selling abroad existed no longer because of the lack of buyers, and it became useless to continue to produce more than the indispensable minimum for the subsis-

[5] The registry of rents of the Abbot Irminon is the principal source of knowledge of this organization. The prolegomena of Guérard in the edition which he issued in 1844, should, however, be read. One should also consult, on this point, the famous *Capitulare de Villis*. K. Gareis has issued a good commentary: *Die Landguterordnung Karls des Grossen,* Berlin, 1895. On the recent controversies over the import and the date of the *Capitulare*, see M. Bloch, "L'origine et la date du Capitulare de Villis," *Revue Historique,* 1923, Vol. CXLIII, p. 40.

tence of the men, proprietors or tenants, living on
the estate.

For an economy of exchange was substituted
an economy of consumption. Each demesne, in
place of continuing to deal with the outside, constituted from this time on a little world of its own.
It lived by itself and for itself, in the traditional
immobility of a patriarchal form of government.
The ninth century is the golden age of what we
have called the closed domestic economy and
which we might call, with more exactitude, the
economy of no markets.[6]

This economy, in which production had no
other aim than the sustenance of the demesnial
group and which in consequence was absolutely
foreign to the idea of profit, can not be considered
as a natural and spontaneous phenomenon. It
was, on the contrary, merely the result of an evolution which forced it to take this characteristic
form. The great proprietors did not give up selling the products of their lands of their own free

[6] Certain authors have believed that demesnial products were
destined for sale. See, for example, F. Keutgen, *Ämter und Zünfte*,
Jena, 1903, p. 58. It is a fact that in certain exceptional cases and,
for example, in times of famine, selling took place. But as a general
rule there was certainly no selling. The texts alleged to prove the
contrary are too few in number and too ambiguous to carry conviction. It is evident that the whole economy of the demesnial
system of the early Middle Ages is in flagrant opposition to this
idea of profit.

will; they stopped because they could not do otherwise. Certainly if commerce had continued to supply them regularly with the means of disposing of these products abroad, they would not have neglected to profit thereby. They did not sell because they could not sell, and they could not sell because markets were wanting. The closed demesnial organization, which made its appearance at the beginning of the ninth century, was a phenomenon due to compulsion. That is merely to say that it was an abnormal phenomenon.

This can be most effectively shown by comparing the picture, which Carolingian Europe presents, with that of Southern Russia at the same era.

We know that bands of sea-faring Norsemen, that is to say of Scandinavians originally from Sweden, established their domination over the Slavs of the watershed of the Dnieper during the course of the ninth century. These conquerors, whom the conquered designated by the name of Russians, naturally had to congregate in groups in order to insure their safety in the midst of the populations they had subjected.

For this purpose they built fortified enclosures, called *gorods* in the Slavic tongue, where they settled with their princes and the images of their gods. The most ancient Russian cities owe their

origin to these entrenched camps. There were such
camps at Smolensk, Suzdal and Novgorod; the
most important and the most civilized was at Kiev,
the prince of which ranked above all the other
princes. The subsistence of the invaders was assured by tributes levied on the native population.

It was therefore possible for the Russians to
live off the land, without seeking abroad to supplement the resources which the country gave
them in abundance. They would have done so,
without doubt, and been content to use the prestations of their subjects if they had found it impossible, like their contemporaries in Western
Europe, to communicate with the exterior. But
the position which they occupied must have early
led them to practise an economy of exchange.

Southern Russia was placed, as a matter of fact,
between two regions of a superior civilization. To
the east, beyond the Caspian Sea, extended the
Caliphate of Bagdad; to the south, the Black Sea
bathed the coasts of the Byzantine Empire and
pointed the way towards Constantinople. The barbarians felt at once the effect of these two strong
centers of attraction. To be sure, they were in the
highest degree energetic, enterprising and adven-
turous, but their native qualities only served to
turn circumstances to the best account. Arab merchants, Jews, and Byzantines were already fre-

quenting the Slavic regions when they took possession, and showed them the route to follow. They
themselves did not hesitate to plunge along it under the spur of the love of gain, quite as natural to
primitive man as to civilized.

The country they occupied placed at their disposal products particularly well suited for trade
with rich empires accustomed to the refinements of
life. Its immense forests furnished them with a
quantity of honey, precious in those days when
sugar was still unknown, and furs, sumptuous-
ness in which was a requisite, even in southern
climes, of luxurious dress and equipment.

Slaves were easier still to procure and, thanks
to the Moslem harems and the great houses or
Byzantine workshops, had a sale as sure as it was
remunerative. Thus as early as the ninth century,
while the Empire of Charlemagne was kept in isolation after the closing of the Mediterranean,
Southern Russia on the contrary was induced to
sell her products in the two great markets which
exercised their attraction on her. The paganism of
the Scandinavians of the Dnieper left them free of
the religious scruples which prevented the Christians of the west from having dealings with the
Moslems. Belonging neither to the faith of Christ
nor to that of Mahomet, they only asked to get

rich, in dealing impartially with the followers of either.

The importance of the trade which they kept up as much with the Moslem Empire as with the Greek, is made clear by the extraordinary number of Arab and Byzantine coins discovered in Russia and which mark, like a golden compass needle, the direction of the commercial routes.

In the region of Kiev they followed to the south the course of the Dnieper, to the east the Volga, and to the north the direction marked by the Western Dvina or the lakes which abut the Gulf of Bothnia. Information from Jewish or Arab travellers and from Byzantine writers fortunately supplements the data from archaeological records. It will suffice here to give a brief résumé of what Constantine Porphyrogenetus reports in the ninth century. He shows the Russians assembling their boats at Kiev each year after the ice melts. Their flotilla slowly descends the Dnieper, whose numerous cataracts present obstacles that have to be avoided by dragging the barks along the banks. The sea once reached, they sail before the wind along the coasts towards Constantinople, the supreme goal of their long and perilous voyage. There the Rusian merchants had a special quarter and made commercial treaties, the oldest of which dates back to the ninth century, regulating their relations with the population. Many of them, seduced by its attractions, settled down there and took service in the Imperial Guard, as had done, before that time, the Germans in the legions of Rome.

The City of the Emperors (*Czarograd*) had for the Russians a fascination the influence of which has lasted across the centuries. It was from her that they received Christianity (957-1015); it was from her that they borrowed their art, their writing, the use of money and a good part of their administrative organization. Nothing more is needed to demonstrate the rôle played by Byzantine commerce in their social life. It occupied so essential a place therein that without it their civilization would remain inexplicable. To be sure, the forms in which it is found are very primitive, but the important thing is not the forms of this traffic; it is the effect it had.

Among the Russians of the late Middle Ages it actually determined the constitution of society. By striking contrast with what has been shown to be the case with their contemporaries of Carolingian Europe, not only the importance but the very idea of real estate was unknown to them. Their notion of wealth comprised only personal property, of which slaves were the most valuable. They

were not interested in land except in so far as, by
their control of it, they were able to appropriate its
products. And if this conception was that of a
class of warrior-conquerors, there is but little
doubt that it was held for so long because these
warriors were, at the same time, merchants. We
might, incidentally, add that the concentration of
the Russians in the *gorods,* motivated in the beginning by military necessity, is itself found to
fit in admirably with commercial needs. An organization created by barbarians for the purpose
of keeping conquered populations under the yoke
was well adapted to the sort of life which theirs
became after they gave heed to the economic attraction of Byzantium and Bagdad. Their example shows that a society does not necessarily have
to pass through an agrarian stage before giving
itself over to commerce. Here commerce appears
as an original phenomenon. And if this is so, it
is because the Russians instead of finding themselves isolated from the outside world like Western Europe were on the contrary pushed or, to
use a better word, *drawn* into contact with it from
the beginning. Out of this derive the violent contrasts which are disclosed in comparing their social state with that of the Carolingian Empire: in
place of a demesnial aristocracy, a commercial

aristocracy; in place of serfs bound to the soil, slaves considered as instruments of work; in place of a population living in the country, a population gathered together in towns; in place, finally, of a simple economy of consumption, an economy of exchange and a regular and permanent commercial activity.

That these outstanding contrasts were the result of circumstances which gave Russia markets while depriving the Carolingian Empire of them, history clearly demonstrates. The activity of Russian trade was maintained, indeed, only as long as the routes to Constantinople and Bagdad remained open before it. It was not fated to withstand the crisis which the Petchenegs brought about in the eleventh century. The invasion of these barbarians along the shores of the Caspian and the Black Seas brought in their train consequences identical to those which the invasion of Islam in the Mediterranean had had for Western Europe in the eighth century.

Just as the latter cut the communications between Gaul and the East, the former cut the communications between Russia and her foreign markets. And in both quarters, the results of this interruption coincide with a singular exactitude. In Russia as in Gaul, when means of communication disappeared and towns were depopulated and the populace forced to find near at hand the means of their subsistence, a period of agricultural economy was substituted for a period of commercial economy. Despite the differences in details, it was the same picture in both cases. The regions of the south, ruined and troubled by the barbarians, gave way in importance to the regions of the north. Kiev fell into a decline as Marseilles had fallen, and the center of the Russian State was removed to Moscow just as the center of the Frankish State, with the Carolingian dynasty, had been removed to the watershed of the Rhine. And to end by making the parallel still more conclusive, there arose, in Russia as in Gaul, a landed aristocracy, and a demesnial system was organized in which the impossibility of exporting or of selling forced production to be limited to the needs of the proprietor and his peasants.

So, in both cases, the same causes produced the same effects. But they did not produce them at the same date. Russia was living by trade at an era when the Carolingian Empire knew only the demesnial régime, and she in turn inaugurated this form of government at the very moment when Western Europe, having found new markets, broke away from it. We shall examine further how this break was accomplished. It will suffice for the moment to have proved, by the example of Russia, the theory that the economy of the Carolingian era was not the result of an internal evolution but must be attributed to the closing of the Mediterranean by Islam.

Chapter III

CITY ORIGINS

A N interesting question is whether or not cities existed in the midst of that essentially agricultural civilization into which Western Europe had developed in the course of the ninth century. The answer depends on the meaning given to the word "city." If by it is meant a locality the population of which, instead of living by cultivating the soil, devotes itself to commercial activity, the answer will have to be "No." The answer will also be in the negative if we understand by "city" a community endowed with legal entity and possessing laws and institutions peculiar to itself. On the other hand, if we think of a city as a center of administration and as a fortress, it is clear that the Carolingian period knew nearly as many cities as the centuries which followed it must have known. That is merely another way of saying that the cities which were then to be found were without two of the fundamental attributes of the cities of the Middle Ages and of modern times—a middle-class population and a communal organization.

Primitive though it may be, every stable society feels the need of providing its members with centers of assembly, or meeting places. Observance of religious rites, maintenance of markets, and political and judicial gatherings necessarily bring about the designation of localities intended for the assembly of those who wish to or who must participate therein.

Military needs have a still more positive effect. Populations have to prepare refuges where will be found momentary protection from the enemy in case of invasion. War is as old as humanity, and the construction of fortresses almost as old as war. The first buildings erected by man seem, indeed, to have been protecting walls. Even today, there is hardly a barbaric race among whom this tendency is not found and, as far back as we may go in the past, the situation remains the same. The *acropoles* of the Greeks, the *oppida* of the Etruscans, the Latins, and the Gauls, the *burgen* of the Germans, the *gorods* of the Slavs, like the *kraals* of the Negroes of South Africa, were in the beginning no more than places of assembly and, especially, of protection. Their plan and their construction depended naturally upon the conformation of the terrain and upon the building materials at hand. But the general arrangement of them was everywhere the same. It consisted of a space,

square or circular in shape, surrounded by ramparts made of trunks of trees, or mud or blocks
of stone, protected by a moat and entered by gates.
In short, it was an enclosure. And it is an interesting fact that the words which in modern English and in modern Russian (*town* and *gorod*)
designate a city, originally designated an enclosure.

In ordinary times, these enclosures remained
empty. The people resorted to them only on the occasion of religious or civic ceremonies, or when
war constrained them to seek refuge there with
their herds. But, little by little with the march of
civilization, their intermittent animation became a
continuous animation. Temples arose; magistrates or chieftains established their residence;
merchants and artisans came to settle. What first
had been only an occasional center of assembly
became a city, the administrative, religious, political and economic center of all the territory of
the tribe whose name it customarily took.

This explains why, in many societies and particularly in classic antiquity, the political life of
the cities was not restricted to the circumference
of their walls. The city, indeed, had been built
for the tribe, and every man in it, whether dwell-
ing within or without the walls, was equally a
citizen thereof. Neither Greece nor Rome knew
anything analogous to the strictly local and par-

ticularist bourgeoisie of the Middle Ages. The life of the city was blended with the national life. The law of the city was, like the religion itself of the city, common to all the people whose capital it was and who constituted with it a single autonomous republic.

The municipal system, then, was identified in antiquity with the constitutional system. And when Rome extended her dominion over all the Mediterranean world, she made it the basis of the administrative system of her Empire. This system withstood, in Western Europe, the Germanic invasions.[1] Vestigial but thoroughly definite relics of it were still to be found in Gaul, in Spain, in Africa, and in Italy, long after the fifth century. Little by little, however, the increasing weakness of social organization did away with most of its characteristic features. By the eighth century, neither the *decuriones,* nor the *gesta municipalia,* nor the *defensor civitatis* were longer in existence. At the same time the thrust of Islam in the Mediterranean, in making impossible the commerce which up to now had still sustained a certain activity in the cities, condemned them to an inevitable decline. But it did not condemn them to death. Curtailed and weakened though they were, they survived. Their social function

[1] See above, Chap. I.

did not altogether disappear. In the agricultural social order of the time, they retained in spite of everything a fundamental importance. It is necessary to take full count of the rôle they played, in order to understand what was to befall them later.

As has been stated above, the Church had based its diocesan boundaries on the boundaries of the Roman cities.[2] Held in respect by the barbarians, it therefore continued to maintain, after their occupation of the provinces of the Empire, the municipal system upon which it had been based. The dying out of trade and the exodus of foreign merchants had no influence on the ecclesiastical organization. The cities where the bishops resided became poorer and less populous without the bishops themselves feeling the effects. On the contrary, the more that general prosperity declined, the more their power and their influence had a chance to assert itself. Endowed with a prestige which was the greater because the State had disappeared, sustained by donations from their congregations, and partners with the Carolingians in the governing of society, they were in a commanding position by virtue of, at one and the same time, their moral authority, their economic power, and their political activity.

[2] See above, Chap. I.

When the Empire of Charlemagne foundered, their status, far from being adversely affected, was made still more secure. The feudal princes, who had destroyed the power of the monarchy, did not touch that of the Church, for its divine origin protected it from their attacks. They feared the bishops who could fling at them the terrible weapon of excommunication. They revered them as the supernatural guardians of order and justice. In the midst of the anarchy of the tenth and eleventh centuries the ascendancy of the Church remained, therefore, unimpaired, and it appeared to merit that good fortune. To combat the plague of the private wars which the Crown was now incapable of repressing, the bishops organized in their dioceses the institution of the "Truce of God."

This prestige of the bishops naturally lent to their places of residence—that is to say, to the old Roman cities—considerable importance. It is highly probable that this was what saved them. In the economy of the ninth century they no longer had any excuse for existence. In ceasing to be commercial centers they must have lost, quite evidently, the greatest part of their population. The merchants who once frequented them, or dwelt there, disappeared and with them disappeared the urban character which they had still

preserved during the Merovingian era. Lay society no longer had the least use for them. Round
about them the great demesnes lived their own
life. There is no evidence that the State, itself constituted on a purely agrarian basis, had any cause
to be interested in their fate. It is quite characteristic, and quite illuminating, that the palaces
(*palatia*) of the Carolingian princes were not located in the towns. They were, without exception,
in the country, in the demesnes of the dynasty:
at Herstal, at Jupille, at Meersen in the valley of
the Meuse; at Ingelheim in that of the Rhine; at
Attigny in that of the Seine; and so on.

The fame of Aix-la-Chapelle should not lead
to any illusion as to the character of that locality.
The resplendency in which it temporarily gloried
under Charlemagne was due only to its fortune
in being the favorite residence of the emperor.
After the reign of Louis the Pious, it fell back
into insignificance. It was to become a real city
only four centuries later.

The State, on its part, in exercising administrative powers could contribute in no way to the
continued existence of the Roman cities. The counties which formed the political districts of the
Empire were without their chief-towns, just as the
Empire itself was without a capital. The counts,
to whom the supervision of them was entrusted,

did not settle down in any fixed spot. They were constantly travelling about their districts in order to preside over judicial assemblies, to levy taxes, and to raise troops. The centers of their administrations were not their places of residence but their persons. It was therefore of little importance whether they had or did not have their domicile in a town. Recruited from among the great proprietors of the region, they were, after all, most accustomed to live on their estates. Their châteaux, like the palaces of the emperors, were customarily in the country.[3]

On the contrary, the immobility which ecclesiastical discipline enforced upon a bishop permanently held him to the city where was established the see of his particular diocese. Though they had lost their function in civil administration, the cities therefore continued to serve as the key points in religious administration. Each diocese comprised the territory about the city which contained its cathedral, and kept in constant touch with it. The change in meaning of the word *civitas* from the beginning of the ninth century throws interesting light on this point. It became synonymous with the bishopric and the episcopal city. The

[3] This is particularly true for Northern Europe. In Southern France and in Italy, on the contrary, where the Roman municipal organization had less completely disappeared, the counts ordinarily lived in the towns.

phrase *civitas Parisiensis* was used to designate the diocese of Paris as well as the city of Paris itself, where the bishop had his residence. Thus under this double connotation was preserved the memory of the ancient municipal system adopted by the Church for her own ends.

In short, what happened in the empoverished and depopulated Carolingian towns is a striking parallel of what, in a rather more important theater, happened at Rome itself when, in the course of the fourth century, the Eternal City had ceased to be the capital of the world. In leaving it for Ravenna and then for Constantinople, the emperors abandoned it to the Pope. What it no longer was in the government of the State, it continued to be in the government of the Church.

The imperial city became the pontifical city. Its historical prestige enhanced that of the successor of St. Peter. Isolated, he seemed the greater, and he became at the same time more powerful. Men now saw only him; in the absence of the old rulers, men now obeyed only him. By continuing to dwell in Rome, he made it *his* Rome, just as each bishop made the city where he dwelt *his* city.

During the last days of the Lower Empire, and still more during the Merovingian era, the power of the bishops over the city populace consistently increased. They had profited by the growing disorganization of civil society to accept, or to arrogate to themselves, an authority which the inhabitants did not take pains to dispute with them, and which the State had no interest in and, moreover, no means of denying them. The privileges which the clergy began to enjoy after the fourth century, in the matters of jurisdiction and taxes, enhanced still further their status. It became more conspicuous through the granting of charters of immunity which the Frankish kings issued in their favor. By virtue of these the bishops were freed from the interference of the counts in their ecclesiastical demesnes. They were invested from that time on— the eighth century—with a complete suzerainty over their people and their lands. To the ecclesiastical jurisdiction over the clergy which they already had was added lay jurisdiction, entrusted to a tribunal, created by them, whose principal seat was fixed, naturally, in the town where they had their residence.

When the disappearance of trade, in the ninth century, annihilated the last vestiges of city life and put an end to what still remained of a municipal population, the influence of the bishops, already so extensive, became unrivalled. Henceforward the towns were entirely under their control. In them were to be found, in fact, practically

only inhabitants dependent more or less directly
upon the Church.

Though no precise information is available, it
is, nevertheless, possible to conjecture as to the
nature of this population. It was composed of the
clerics of the cathedral church and of the other
churches grouped nearby; of the monks of the
monasteries which, especially after the ninth century, came to be established, sometimes in great
numbers, in the see of the diocese; of the teachers
and the students of the ecclesiastical schools; and
finally, of servitors and artisans, free or serf, who
were indispensable to the needs of the religious
group and to the daily existence of the clerical
agglomeration.

Almost always there was to be found in the
town a weekly market whither the peasants from
roundabout brought their produce. Sometimes,
even, an annual fair was held there. At the gates
a market toll was levied on everything that came
in or went out. A mint was in operation within
the walls. There were also to be found there a
number of keeps occupied by vassals of the bishop,
by his advocate or by his castellan. To all of this
must be added, finally, the granaries and the store-
houses where were stored the harvests from the
monastical demesnes brought in, at stated periods,
by the tenant-farmers. At the great yearly festi-

vals the congregation of the diocese poured into the town and gave it, for several days, the animation of unaccustomed bustle and stir.[4]

All this little world accepted the bishop as both its spiritual and temporal head. Religious and secular authority were united or, to put it better, were blended in his person. Aided by a Council formed of priests and canons, he administered the city and the diocese in conformity with the precepts of Christian morality. His ecclesiastical tribune, presided over by the archdeacon, had singularly enlarged its sphere, thanks to the impotency, and still more to the favor, of the State. Not only were all the clerics subject to it in every particular, but to it also pertained jurisdiction over a number of matters affecting the laity: matters of marriage, of wills, of civil position, etc. The province of the lay court, which was presided over either by the castellan or the advocate, had profited by a similar increase in scope. After the reign of Louis the Pious its jurisdiction had been enlarged by gradual infringements which the more

---

[4] The towns of the ninth and tenth centuries have not yet been adequately studied. What is said of them here, and later, is borrowed from various passages in the capitularies as well as from certain scattered texts in the chronicles and the lives of the Saints. For the towns of Germany, unfortunately much less numerous and less important than those of Gaul, the reader should consult the interesting work of S. Rietschel, *Die Civitas auf deutschem Boden bis zum Ausgange der Karolingerzeit*, Leipzig, 1894.

and more flagrant disorders of the public administration explain and justify. Those affected by
the charters of immunity were not the only ones
subject thereto. It seems quite certain that, at least
within the actual limits of the town, everybody
came under its jurisdiction and that it had been
substituted, *in fact,* for the jurisdiction which the
count still possessed, *in theory,* over the freemen.[5]
In addition, the bishop enjoyed very loosely defined police powers, under which he supervised
the markets, regulated the levying of tolls, took
care of the bridges and the ramparts. In short,
there was no longer any field in the administration of the town wherein, whether by law or by
prerogative, he did not intervene as the guardian
of order, peace, and the common weal. A theo-
cratic form of government had completely replaced the municipal regimen of antiquity. The
populace was governed by its bishop and no
longer asked to have even the least share in that
government. True, it sometimes happened that a
disturbance broke out in the town. Bishops were
assailed in their palaces and sometimes even
obliged to flee. But it is stretching a point to find in
these events the least trace of a municipal spirit.

[5] I am seeking, naturally, to characterize only the general situation. I am aware that numerous exceptions must be made; but
they cannot modify the general impression which comes from an
examination of the data available.

They are rather to be explained by intrigues or personal rivalries.

It would be thoroughly fallacious to consider them the precursors of the communal movement of the eleventh and twelfth centuries. Moreover, they were very rare. Everything indicates that the episcopal administration was in general beneficent and popular.

This administration, as pointed out above, was not confined to the limits of the town. It extended throughout the bishopric. The town was its center, but the diocese was its sphere. Under it the urban population enjoyed in no particular a privileged status. The regimen under which it lived was the regimen of the common law. The knights, the serfs, and the freemen whom it contained were distinguished from their congeners outside only by being grouped in one locality. Of the special laws and the autonomy which the bourgeoisie of the Middle Ages was to enjoy, there was not yet a single trace to be discovered. The word *civis* (citizen) by which contemporary texts designated the inhabitant of the town was only a simple topographical appellation; it did not yet have legal significance.

These towns were fortresses as well as episcopal residences. In the last days of the Roman Empire they had been enclosed by walls as a protection against the barbarians. These walls were still in existence almost everywhere and the bishops busied themselves with keeping them up or with restoring them with the greater zeal in that the incursions of the Saracens and the Norsemen had given increasingly impressive proof, during the ninth century, of the need of protection. The old Roman enclosures continued, therefore, to protect the towns against new perils.

Their form remained, under Charlemagne, what it had been under Constantine. As a general rule, it took the shape of a rectangle surrounded by ramparts flanked by towers and communicating with the outside by gates, customarily to the number of four. The space so enclosed was very restricted and the length of its sides rarely exceeded four to five hundred yards. Moreover, it was far from being entirely built up; between the houses cultivated fields and gardens were to be found. The outskirts (*suburbium*), which in the Merovingian era still extended beyond the walls, had disappeared. Thanks to their defenses, the towns could almost always victoriously oppose the assaults of the invaders from the north and the south. It will suffice here to recall the famous siege of Paris by the Norsemen in 885.

The episcopal cities naturally served as a refuge for the populations of their neighborhood upon the approach of the barbarians. There monks came, even from very far away, to seek an asylum, as did, for example, those from St. Vaast in 887 at Beauvais and those from St. Quentin at Laon.

In the midst of the insecurity and the disorders which imparted so lugubrious a character to the second half of the ninth century, it therefore fell to the towns to fulfill a true mission of protection. They were, in every sense of the word, the ramparts of a society invaded, under tribute, and terrorized. Soon, from another cause, they were not to be alone in filling that rôle.

It is obvious that the anarchy of the ninth century hastened the inevitable decomposition of the Frankish State. The counts, who were the biggest proprietors of their districts, profited by existing conditions to arrogate to themselves a complete autonomy, to make of their office an hereditary estate, to combine in their hands, with the private powers they exercised over their own demesnes, the public powers which were delegated to them, and finally to amalgamate under their domination, in a single principality, all the counties they could lay hold of. The Carolingian Empire was thus parcelled out, after the middle of the ninth century, into a number of territories subject to as many local dynasties, and attached to the Crown only by the fragile bond of feudal homage.

The State was too feeble to resist this disintegration. It was accomplished, unquestionably, by means of violence and abominable perfidies. Nevertheless it was, on the whole, beneficial for society. In seizing power, the princes forthwith accepted the obligations it imposed. Their most evident interest was to defend and protect the lands and the people who had become *their* lands and *their* people. They did not fail in a task which a purely selfish concern for personal power had imposed upon them. As their power grew and was consolidated, they became more and more preoccupied with giving their principalities an organization capable of guaranteeing public order and peace.

The first need which was manifest was that of defense, as much against the Saracens or the Norsemen as against the neighboring princes. Fortresses, therefore, sprang up everywhere at the beginning of the ninth century.[6] Contemporary texts give them the most diverse names: *castellum, castrum, oppidum, urbs, municipium*; the most usual and in any case the most technical of these appellations is that of *burgus,* a word borrowed from the German by the Latin of the Lower Em-

[6] Before the arrival of the Norsemen, there were not any, or hardly any, fortified localities outside of the episcopal cities. Hariulphe, *Chronique de l'abbaye de Saint-Riquier,* edit. F. Lot, Paris, 1894, p. 118.

pire and which is preserved in all the modern languages: *burg, borough, bourg, borgo.*[7]

Of these burgs of the late Middle Ages no trace remains in our day. The sources of information, however, fortunately make it possible to form a fairly accurate picture of them. They were walled enclosures of somewhat restricted perimeter, customarily circular in form and surrounded by a moat. In the center was to be found a strong-tower and a keep, the last redoubt of defense in case of attack. A permanent garrison of knights (*milites castrenses*) was kept stationed there. This was placed under the orders of a castellan (*castellanus*). The prince had a home (*domus*) in each of the burgs of his territory where he stayed with his retinue in the course of the continual changes of residence which war or administerial duties forced upon him. Very often a chapel, or a church flanked by the buildings necessary to house the clergy, raised its belfry above the battlements of the rampart. Sometimes there were also to be found by the side of it quarters intended for the judicial assemblies whose members came, at fixed periods, from outside to assemble in the burg. Finally, what was never lacking were a granary and cellars

[7] On the meaning of these words, see K. Hegel, *Neues Archiv der Gesellschaft für ältere deutsche Geschichtskunde,* 1892, Vol. XVIII, and G. Des Marez, "Le sens juridique du mot oppidum," *Festschrift für H. Brunner,* Berlin, 1910.

where was kept, to supply the necessities of a siege should the case arise and to furnish subsistence to the prince during his stays, the produce of the neighboring demesnes which he held. Prestations in kind levied on the peasants of the district assured the subsistence of the garrison, on its part. The upkeep of the walls devolved upon these same peasants who were compelled to do the work by statute labor.

Although from country to country the picture, which has just been drawn, naturally differed in details, the same essential traits were to be found everywhere. The similarity between the *bourgs* of Flanders and the *boroughs* of Anglo-Saxon England is a striking one.[8] And this similarity unquestionably proves that the same needs brought in their train like results everywhere.

As can be easily seen, the burgs were, above all, military establishments. But to this original func-

[8] F. W. Maitland, *Township and Borough,* 1898. The reader should also compare the burgs of the west with those built in the tenth century as a defense against the Slavs, along the Elbe and the Saale, by Henry the Fowler. D. Schäfer, "Die Milites agrarii des Witukinds," *Abhandlungen der Berliner Akademie,* 1905, p. 572. For the social rôle of the burgs, we restrict ourselves to citing the following text which seems to be thoroughly characteristic; it had to do with the founding in 996 of Cateau-Cambrésis: "*ut esset obstaculum latronibus praesidiumque libertatis circum et circa rusticanis cultoribus.*" "Gesta episcoporum Cameracensium," *Monumenta Germaniae Historica,* Vol. VII, p. 450.

tion was early added that of being administrative centers. The castellan ceased to be solely the commandant of the knights of the castral garrison. The prince delegated to him financial and juridical authority over a more or less extensive district round about the walls of the burg and which took, by the tenth century, the name of castellany. The castellany was related to the burg as the bishopric was related to the town. In case of war, its inhabitants found there a refuge; in time of peace, there they repaired to take part in the assemblies of justice or to pay off the prestations to which they were subject. Nevertheless the burg did not show the slightest urban character. Its population comprised, aside from the knights and the clerics who made up its essential part, only men employed in their service and whose number was certainly of very little importance. It was a fortress population; it was not a city population. Neither commerce nor industry was possible or even conceivable in such an environment. It produced nothing of itself, lived by revenues from the surrounding country, and had no other economic rôle than that of a simple consumer.

It is therefore a safe conclusion that the period which opened with the Carolingian era knew cities neither in the social sense, nor in the economic sense, nor in the legal sense of that word. The towns and the burgs were merely fortified places and headquarters of administration. Their inhabitants enjoyed neither special laws nor institutions of their own, and their manner of living did not distinguish them in any way from the rest of society.

Commercial and industrial activity were completely foreign to them. In no respect were they out of key with the agricultural civilization of their times. The groups they formed were, after all, of trifling importance. It is not possible, in the lack of reliable information, to give an exact figure, but everything indicates that the population of the burgs never consisted of more than a few hundred men and that that of the towns probably did not pass the figure of two to three thousand souls.

The towns and the burgs played, however, an essential rôle in the history of cities. They were, so to speak, the stepping-stones thereto. Round about their walls cities were to take shape after the economic renaissance, whose first symptoms appeared in the course of the tenth century, had made itself manifest.

Chapter IV

The Revival of Commerce

THE end of the ninth century was the moment when the economic development of Western Europe that followed the closing of the Mediterranean was at its lowest ebb. It was also the moment when the social disorganization caused by the raids of the barbarians and the accompanying political anarchy reached a maximum.

The tenth century, if not an era of recovery, was at least an era of stabilization and relative peace. The surrender of Normandy to Rollo (912) marked in the west the end of the great Scandinavian invasions, while in the east Henry the Fowler and Otto I checked and held the Slavs along the Elbe and the Hungarians in the valley of the Danube (934, 955). At the same time the feudal system, which had definitely displaced the monarchy, was established in France on the débris of the old Carolingian order. In Germany, on the contrary, the somewhat later development of society enabled the princes of the House of Saxony to resist the encroachments of the lay aristocracy.

On their side they had the powerful influence of the bishops and used it to restore the ascendancy of the monarchy. In assuming the title of Roman Emperor, they laid claim to the universal authority which Charlemagne had exercised.

If all this was not accomplished without bitter conflicts, nevertheless it was decidedly productive of good. Europe ceased to be overrun by ruthless hordes. She recovered confidence in the future, and, with that confidence, courage and ambition. The date of the renewal of a cooperative activity on the part of the people might well be ascribed to the tenth century. At that date, likewise, the social authorities began once more to acquit themselves in the rôle which it was their place to play. From now on, in feudal as well as in episcopal principalities, the first traces could be seen of an organized effort to better the condition of the people. The prime need of that era, hardly rising above anarchy, was the need of peace, the most fundamental and the most essential of all the needs of society.

The first Truce of God was proclaimed in 989. Private wars, the greatest of the plagues that harassed those troubled times, were energetically combated by the territorial counts in France and by the prelates of the imperial Church in Germany.

Dark though the prospect still was, the tenth century nevertheless saw in outline the picture which the eleventh century presents. The famous legend of the terrors of the year 1000 is not devoid, in this respect, of symbolic significance. It is doubtless untrue that men expected the end of the world in the year 1000. Yet the century which came in at that date is characterized, in contrast with the preceding one, by a recrudescence of activity so marked that it could pass for the vigorous and joyful awakening of a society long oppressed by a nightmare of anguish. In every demesne was to be seen the same burst of energy and, for that matter, of optimism. The Church, revivified by the Clunisian reform, undertook to purify herself of the abuses which had crept into her discipline and to shake off the bondage in which the emperors held her. A mystic enthusiasm of which she was the inspiration, animated her congregations and launched them upon the heroic and grandiose enterprise of the Crusades which brought Western Christianity to grips with Islam. The military spirit of feudalism led her to initiate and to succeed in epic undertakings. Norman knights went to battle with Byzantines and Moslems in Southern Italy, and founded there the principalities out of which was later to arise the Kingdom of Sicily; other Normans, with whom were associated Flemings and Frenchmen from the north, conquered England under the leadership of Duke William. South of the Pyrenees the Christians drove before them the Saracens of Spain; Toledo and Valencia fell to their hands (1072-1109).

Such undertakings testify not only to energy and vigor of spirit; they testify also to the health of society. They would have obviously been impossible without that native strength which is one of the characteristics of the eleventh century. The fecundity of families seemed, at this date, to be as general among the nobility as among the peasants. Younger sons abounded everywhere, feeling themselves crowded for room on their natal soil and eager to try their fortunes abroad. Everywhere were to be met adventurers in search of money or work. The armies were full of mercenaries, "Coterelli" or "Brabantiones," letting their services to whoever wished to employ them. From Flanders and Holland bands of peasants were setting out, by the beginning of the twelfth century, to drain the *Mooren* on the banks of the Elbe. In every part of Europe labor was offered in superabundant quantity and this is undoubtedly the explanation of the increasing number, from then on, of great reclamation projects in clearing land and diking streams.

It does not appear that, from the Roman era to the eleventh century, the area of cultivated land had been perceptibly increased. Save in the Germanic countries, the monasteries had hardly altered, in this respect, the existing situation. They were almost always established on old estates and did nothing to decrease the extent of the woods, the heaths and the marshes contained within their demesnes. But it was quite a different matter when once the increase of population permitted these unproductive terrains to be put to good use. Just about the year 1000 there began a period of reclamation which was to continue, with steady increase, up to the end of the twelfth century. Europe "colonized" herself, thanks to the increase of her inhabitants. The princes and the great proprietors turned to the founding of new towns, where flocked the "younger sons" in quest of lands to cultivate. The great forests began to be cleared. In Flanders appeared, about 1150, the first *polders*. (A "polder" is diked land, reclaimed from the sea.) The Order of the Cistercians, founded in 1098, gave itself over at once to reclamation projects and the clearing of the land.

It is easy to see that the increase in population and the burst of renewed general activity of which it was both cause and effect, operated from the very first to the benefit of an agricultural economy.

But this condition should, before long, have had its effect upon trade as well. The eleventh century, in fact, brings us face to face with a real commercial revival. This revival received its impetus from two centers of activity, one located in the south and the other in the north: Venice on one side and the Flemish coast on the other. And this is merely another way of saying that it was the result of an external stimulus. The contact with foreign trade, maintained at these two points, first caused it to appear and spread. Quite likely it could have come about in some other way. Commercial activity might have been revived by virtue of the trend of general economic life. The fact is, however, that this was not the case. Just as the trade of the west disappeared with the shutting off of its foreign markets, just so it was renewed when these markets were reopened.

Venice, whose influence was felt from the very first, has a well recognized and singular place in the economic history of Europe. Like Tyre, Venice shows an exclusively commercial character. Her first inhabitants, fleeing before the approach of the Huns, the Goths and the Lombards, had sought (in the fifth and sixth centuries) a refuge on the barren islets of the lagoons at Rialto, at Olivolo, at Spinalunga, at Dorsoduro. To exist in these marshes they had to tax their ingenuity and to fight against Nature herself. Everything was wanting: even drinking water was lacking. But the sea was enough for the existence of a folk who knew how to manage things. Fishing and the preparation of salt supplied an immediate means of livelihood to the Venetians. They were able to procure wheat by exchanging their products with the inhabitants of the neighbuuring shores.

Trade was thus forced upon them by the very conditions under which they lived. And they had the energy and the genius to turn to profit the unlimited possibilities which trade offered them. By the eighth century the group of islets they occupied was already thickly populated enough to become the see of a special diocese.

At the date when the city was founded, all Italy still belonged to the Byzantine Empire. Thanks to her insular situation, the conquerors who successively overran the peninsula—first the Lombards, then Charlemagne, and finally, still later, the German emperors—were not successful in their attempts to gain possession. She remained, therefore, under the sovereignty of Constantinople, thus forming at the upper end of the Adriatic and at the foot of the Alps an isolated outpost of Byzantine civilization. While Western Europe was detaching herself from the east, she continued to be part of it. And this circumstance is of

capital importance. The consequence was that
Venice did not cease to gravitate in the orbit of
Constantinople. Across the waters, she was subject
to the attraction of that great city and herself grew
great under its influence.

Constantinople, even in the eleventh century,
appears not only as a great city, but as the greatest
city of the whole Mediterranean basin. Her population was not far from reaching the figure of a
million inhabitants, and that population was singularly active. She was not content, as had been
the population of Rome under the Republic and
the Empire, to consume without producing. She
gave herself over, with a zeal which the fiscal system shackled but did not choke, not only to trading but to industry. For Constantinople was a
great port and a first-rate manufacturing center
as well as a political capital. Here were to be
found every manner of life and every form of
social activity. Alone, in the Christian world, she
presented a picture analogous to that of great
modern cities with all the complexities, all the de-
fects but also with all the refinements of an essentially urban civilization. An uninterrupted shipping kept her in touch with the coasts of the Black
Sea, Asia Minor, Southern Italy, and the shores
of the Adriatic. Her war fleets secured to her the
mastery of the sea, without which she would not

have been able to live. As long as she remained
powerful, she was able to maintain, in the face of
Islam, her dominion over all the waters of the
Eastern Mediterranean.

It is easy to understand how Venice profited by
her alliance with a world so different from the
European west. To it she not only owed the prosperity of her commerce, but from it she first
learned those higher forms of civilization, that
perfected technique, that business enterprise, and
that political and administrative organization
which gave her a place apart in the Europe of
the Middle Ages. By the eighth century she was
devoting herself with greater and greater success
to the provisioning of Constantinople. Her ships
transported thither the products of the countries
which were contiguous to her on the east and the
west: wheat and wine from Italy, wood from Dalmatia, salt from the lagoons, and, in spite of the
prohibitions of the Pope and the Emperor himself, slaves which she easily secured among the
Slavic peoples of the shores of the Adriatic.
Thence they brought back, in return, the precious
fabrics of Byzantine manufacture, as well as
spices which Asia furnished to Constantinople.
By the tenth century the activity of the port had
already attained extraordinary proportions. And
with the extension of trade, the love of gain be-

came irresistible. No scruple had any weight with the Venetians. Their religion was a religion of business men. It mattered little to them that the Moslems were the enemies of Christ, if business with them was profitable. After the ninth century they began more and more to frequent Aleppo, Cairo, Damascus, Kairwan, Palermo. Treaties of commerce assured their merchants a privileged status in the markets of Islam.

By the start of the eleventh century, the power of Venice was making as marvellous progress as her wealth. Under the Doge Pietro II Orseolo, she cleared the Adriatic of the Slavic pirates, subjected Istria and had at Zara, Veglia, Arbe, Trau, Spalato, Curzola, and Lagosta settlements or military establishments. John the Deacon extols the splendor and the glory of *Venetia Aurea,* and William of Apuleia vaunts the city "rich in money, rich in men," and declares that "no people in the world are more valorous in naval warfare, more skilful in the art of guiding ships on the sea."

It was inevitable that the powerful economic movement, of which Venice was the center, should be communicated to the countries of Italy from which she was separated only by the lagoons. There she obtained the wheat and wine which she either consumed herself or exported, and she naturally sought to create there a market for the eastern merchandise which her mariners unloaded in greater and greater quantity on the quays by the Po. She entered into relations with Pavia, which was not long in being animated by her infectious activity. She obtained from the German emperors the right to trade freely first with the nearby cities and then with all Italy, as well as the shipping monopoly for all goods arriving in her port.

In the course of the tenth century Lombardy was inspired, by her example, with commercial life. Trade rapidly spread from Pavia to the neighboring cities. All of them made haste to share in the traffic of which Venice had given them the outstanding example and which it was to her interest to stimulate among them. The spirit of enterprise developed in one place after another.

It was not only products of the soil which kept the commercial relations with Venice flourishing. Industry was already commencing to appear. Early in the eleventh century, for example, Lucca turned to the manufacture of cloths and kept at it until much later. Probably a great many more details would be known about the beginnings of this economic revival in Lombardy if our sources of information were not so deplorably meagre.

Preponderant as the Venetian influence had been in Italy, it did not make itself felt there ex-

clusively. The south of the peninsula beyond
Spoleto and Benevento was still, and so remained
until the arrival of the Normans in the eleventh
century, under the power of the Byzantine Empire. Bari, Tarentum, Naples and above all
Amalfi, kept up relations with Constantinople
similar to those of Venice. They were very active
centers of trade and, no more than Venice, did
not hesitate to traffic with Moslem ports.

Their shipping was, naturally, fated to find
competitors sooner or later among the inhabitants
of the coastal towns situated further to the north.
And, in fact, after the beginning of the eleventh
century we see first Genoa, then Pisa soon after,
turning their attention to the sea. In 935 the Saracen pirates had again pillaged Genoa. But the moment was approaching when she was in her turn
to take the offensive. There could be no question
of her concluding commercial arrangements, as
had Venice or Amalfi, with the enemies of her
Faith. The mystic, excessive scrupulousness of
the west in religious matters did not permit it,
and too many hates had accumulated in the course
of the centuries. The sea could be opened up only
by force of arms.

In 1015-1016 an expedition was undertaken
by Genoa, in cooperation with Pisa, against Sar-

dinia. Twenty years later, in 1034, they got possession for a time of Bona on the coast of Africa; the Pisans, on their part, victoriously entered the port of Palermo in 1062 and destroyed its arsenal.

In 1087 the fleets of the two cities, encouraged by Pope Victor III, attacked Mehdia. All these expeditions were due as much to religious enthusiasm as to the spirit of adventure. With a quite different viewpoint from that of the Venetians, the Genoese and the Pisans considered themselves soldiers of Christ and of the Church, opponents of Islam. They believed they saw the Archangel Gabriel and St. Peter leading them into battle with the Infidels, and it was only after having massacred the "priests of Mahomet" and pillaged the mosque of Mehdia that they signed an advantageous treaty of commerce. The Cathedral of Pisa, built after this triumph, admirably symbolized both the mysticism of the conquerors and the wealth which their shipping was beginning to bring to them. Pillars and precious marble brought from Africa served to decorate it—it seems as if they had wished to attest by its splendor the revenge of Christianity upon the Saracens whose opulence was a thing of scandal and of envy. Those, at least, are the sentiments which an enthusiastic contemporary poem expresses:

*Unde tua in aeternum splendebit ecclesia
Auro, gemnis, margaritis et palliis splendida**

Before the counter-attack of Christianity, Islam thus gave way little by little. The launching of the First Crusade (1096) marked its definite recoil. In 1097 a Genoese fleet sailed towards Antioch, bringing to the Crusaders reinforcements and supplies. Two years later Pisa sent out vessels "under the orders of the Pope" to deliver Jerusalem. From that time on the whole Mediterranean was opened, or rather reopened, to western shipping. As in the Roman era, communications were reestablished from one end to the other of that essentially European sea.

The Empire of Islam, in so far as the sea was concerned, came to an end. To be sure, the political and religious results of the Crusade were ephemeral. The kingdom of Jerusalem and the principalities of Edessa and Antioch were reconquered by the Moslems in the twelfth century. But the sea remained in the hands of the Christians. They were the ones who held undisputed economic mastery over it. All the shipping in the ports of the Levant came gradually under their control. Their commercial establishments multiplied with surprising rapidity in the ports of

* "Thy church will be resplendent for eternity,
   Dazzling with gold, with gems, with pearls and precious cloths."

Syria, Egypt and the isles of the Ionian Sea. The conquest of Corsica (1091), of Sardinia (1022) and of Sicily (1058-1090) took away from the Saracens the bases of operations which, since the ninth century, had enabled them to keep the west in a state of blockade. The ships of Genoa and Pisa kept the sea routes open. They patronized the markets of the east, whither came the products of Asia, both by caravan and by the ships of the Red Sea and the Persian Gulf, and frequented in their turn the great port of Byzantium. The capture of Amalfi by the Normans (1073), in putting an end to the commerce of that city, freed them from her rivalry.

But their progress immediately aroused the jealousy of Venice. She could not bear to share with these newcomers a trade in which she laid claim to a monopoly. It was of no moment that she professed the same Faith, belonged to the same people and spoke the same language; since they had become rivals she saw in them only enemies. In the spring of the year 1100 a Venetian squadron, lying in wait before Rhodes for the return of the fleet which Pisa had sent to Jerusalem, fell upon it unawares and ruthlessly sank a large number of vessels. So began between the maritime cities a conflict which was to last as long as their prosperity. The Mediterranean was no more to know that Roman peace which the Empire of the Caesars had once enjoined upon her. The divergence of interests was hereafter to sustain on the sea a hostility, sometimes secret and sometimes openly declared, between the rivals who contested for supremacy. The quarrels of the Italian republics of the Middle Ages are still duplicated in modern times by the continued wrangling of the States whose coasts the Mediterranean washes.

In developing, maritime commerce must naturally have become more generalized. By the beginning of the twelfth century it had reached the shores of France and Spain. After the long stagnation into which the city had fallen at the end of the Merovingian period, the old port of Marseilles took on new life. In Catalonia, Barcelona, out of which the kings of Aragon had driven the Moslems, profited in turn by the opening up of the sea. However, Italy undoubtedly kept the upper hand in that first economic revival. Lombardy, where from Venice on the east and Pisa and Genoa on the west all the commercial movements of the Mediterranean flowed and were blended into one, flourished with an extraordinary exuberance. On that wonderful plain cities bloomed with the same vigor as the harvests. The fertility of the soil made possible for them an unlimited expansion, and at the same time the ease of obtaining markets favored both the importation of raw materials and the exportation of manufactured products. There, commerce gave rise to industry, and as it developed, Bergamo, Cremona, Lodi, Verona, and all the old towns, all the old Roman *municipia,* took on new life, far more vigorous than that which had animated them in antiquity. Soon their surplus production and their fresh energy were seeking to expand abroad. In the south Tuscany was won. In the north new routes were laid out across the Alps. By the passes of the Splügen, St. Bernard and the Brenner, their merchants were to bring to the continent of Europe that same healthy stimulus which had come to them from the sea. They followed those natural routes marked by river courses—the Danube to the east, the Rhine to the north, and the Rhône to the west. In 1074 Italian merchants, undoubtedly Lombards, are made mention of at Paris; and at the beginning of the twelfth century the fairs of Flanders were already drawing a considerable number of their compatriots.

Nothing could be more natural than this appearance of southerners on the Flemish coast. It was a consequence of the attraction which trade spontaneously exerts upon trade.

It has already been shown that, during the Carolingian era, the Netherlands had given evidence of a commercial activity not to be found anywhere else.[1] This is easily explained by the great number of rivers which flow through that country and which there unite their waters before emptying into the sea: the Rhine, the Meuse and the Scheldt. England and the Scandinavian countries were so near that land of large and deep estuaries that their mariners naturally frequented it at an early date. It was to them, as we have seen above, that the ports of Duurstede and Quentovic owed their importance. But this importance was ephemeral. It could not survive the period of the Norseman invasions. The easier access was to a country, the more it lured the invaders and the more it had to suffer from their devastations. The geographical situation which, at Venice, had safeguarded commercial prosperity was, here, naturally due to contribute to its destruction.

The invasions of the Norsemen had been only the first manifestation of the need of expansion felt by the Scandinavian peoples. Their overflowing energy had driven them forth, towards Western Europe and Russia simultaneously, upon adventures of pillage and conquest. They were not mere pirates. They aspired, as had the Germanic

[1] See above, pp. 33-4.

tribes before them with regard to the Roman Empire, to settle in countries more rich and fertile than was their homeland, and there to create colonies for the surplus population which their own country could no longer support. In this undertaking they eventually succeeded. To the east, the Swedes set foot along those natural routes which led from the Baltic to the Black Sea by way of the Neva, Lake Ladoga, the Lovat, the Volchof, the Dvina and the Dnieper. To the west, the Danes and the Norwegians colonized the Anglo-Saxon kingdoms north of the Humber. In France, they had ceded to them by Charles the Simple the country on the Channel which took from them the name of Normandy.

These successes had for their result the orientation in a new direction of the activity of the Scandinavians. Starting at the beginning of the tenth century, they turned away from war to devote themselves to trade. Their ships plowed all the seas of the north and they had nothing to fear from rivals since they alone, among the peoples whose shores those seas bathed, were navigators. It is enough to peruse the delightful tales of the sagas to get an idea of the hardihood and the skill of the barbarian mariners whose adventures and exploits they recount.

Each spring, once the water was open, they put out to sea. They were to be met in Iceland, in Ireland, in England, in Flanders, at the mouths of the Elbe, the Weser, and the Vistula, on the islands of the Baltic Sea, at the head of the Gulf of Bothnia and the Gulf of Finland. They had settlements at Dublin, at Hamburg, at Schwerin, on the island of Gotland; thanks to them, the current of trade, which starting from Byzantium and Bagdad crossed Russia by way of Kiev and Novgorod, was extended up to the shores of the North Sea and there made felt its beneficent influence. In all history there is hardly a more curious phenomenon than that effect wrought on Northern Europe by the superior civilizations of the Greek and Arab Empires, and of which the Scandinavians were the intermediaries. In this respect their rôle, despite the differences of climate, society and culture, seems quite analogous to that which Venice played in the south of Europe. Like her, they renewed the contact between the east and the west. And just as the commercial activity of Venice did not long delay in involving Lombardy in the movement, so likewise Scandinavian shipping brought about the economic awakening of the coast of Flanders.

The geographical situation of Flanders, indeed, put her in a splendid position to become the west-

ern focus for the commerce of the seas of the
north. It formed the natural terminus of the voyage for ships arriving from Northern England or
which, having crossed the Sound after coming out
of the Baltic, were on their way to the south. As
has already been stated, the ports of Quentovic
and Duurstede had been frequented by the Norsemen before the period of the invasions. First one
and then the other disappeared before the storm.
Quentovic did not rise again from her ruins and
it was Bruges, whose situation at the head of the
Gulf of Zwyn was the better one, that became her
heritor. As for Duurstede, Scandinavian mariners
reappeared there at the beginning of the tenth century. Yet her prosperity did not last very long.
As commerce flourished it was concentrated more
and more about Bruges, nearer to France and kept
in a more stable condition of peace by the Counts
of Flanders, whereas the neighborhood of Duurstede was too exposed to the incursions of the still
half-barbaric Friesians to enjoy security. Be that
as it may, it is certain that Bruges attracted to her
port, more and more, the trade of the north, and
that the disappearance of Duurstede, in the course
of the eleventh century, definitely assured her future. The fact that coins of the Counts of Flanders, Arnold II and Baldwin IV (956-1035),
have been discovered in considerable numbers in

Denmark, in Prussia, and even in Russia, would attest, in the lack of written information, to the relations with those countries which Flanders kept up after this date with the help of Scandinavian mariners.

Communication with the nearby English coast was to become still more active. It was at Bruges, for example, that the Anglo-Saxon Queen Emma, expelled from England, settled about 1030. In 991-1002 the list of market tolls at London makes mention of the Flemings as if they were the most important group of foreigners carrying on business in that city.

Among the causes of the commercial importance which so early characterized Flanders, should be pointed out the existence in that country of an indigenous industry able to supply the vessels that landed there with a valuable return cargo. From the Roman era and probably even before that, the Morini and the Menapii had been making woollen cloths. This primitive industry was due to be perfected under the influence of the technical improvements introduced by the Roman conquest. The peculiar fineness of the fleece of the sheep raised on the humid meadows of the coast was the final factor needed to insure success. The tunics (*saga*) and the cloaks (*birri*) which it produced were exported as far as beyond the Alps

and there even was at Tournai, in the last days
of the Empire, a factory for military clothing.
The Germanic invasion did not put an end to this
industry. The Franks who invaded Flanders in
the fifth century continued to carry it on as had
the older inhabitants before them—there is no
doubt but that the Friesian cloaks of which the
ninth century historiographer speaks were made
in Flanders. They seem to be the only manufactured products which furnished, in the Carolingian era, the substance of a regular trade. The
Friesians transported them along the Scheldt, the
Meuse and the Rhine, and when Charlemagne
wanted to reply with gifts to the compliments of
the Caliph Harun-al-Rashid, he found nothing
better to offer him than *"pallia fresonica."* It is
to be supposed that these cloths, as remarkable
for their beautiful colors as for their softness,
must have immediately attracted the attention of
the Scandinavian navigators of the tenth century.
Nowhere, in the north of Europe, were found
more valuable products, and they undoubtedly
had a place, side by side with the furs of the
north and the Arab and Byzantine silk fabrics,
among the most sought-after export goods. According to every indication, the cloths which were
made mention of in the London market about the
year 1000 were cloths from Flanders. And the

new markets which shipping was now offering to them could not have failed to give a fresh impulse to their manufacture.

Thus commerce and industry, the latter carried on locally and the former originating abroad, joined in giving Flanders, after the tenth century, an economic activity that was to continue developing. In the eleventh century the advances made were already surprising. Thenceforth Flanders traded with the north of France the wines of which she exchanged for her cloths. The conquest of England by William of Normandy bound to the Continent that country which heretofore had gravitated in the orbit of Denmark, and multiplied the relations which Bruges had already been maintaining with London. By the side of Bruges, other mercantile centers appeared: Ghent, Ypres, Lille, Douai, Arras, Tournai. Fairs were instituted by the Counts of Thourout at Messines, Lille and Ypres.

Flanders was not alone in experiencing the salutary effects of the shipping of the north. The repercussion made itself felt along the rivers which end in the Netherlands. Cambrai and Valenciennes on the Scheldt, Liège, Huy and Dinant on the Meuse had already, in the tenth century, been mentioned as centers of trade. This was true also of Cologne and Mainz, on the Rhine. The shores of the Channel and of the Atlantic, further removed from the seat of activity of the North Sea, do not seem to have had the same importance. Hardly any mention was made of them, with the exception of Rouen, naturally in close contact with England, and, further south, Bordeaux and Bayonne whose development was much slower. As for the interior of France and Germany, they were affected only very slightly by the economic movement which little by little spread in that direction, either coming up from Italy or coming down from the Netherlands.

It was only in the twelfth century that, gradually but definitely, Western Europe was transformed. The economic development freed her from the traditional immobility to which a social organization, depending solely on the relations of man to the soil, had condemned her. Commerce and industry did not merely find a place alongside of agriculture; they reacted upon it. Its products no longer served solely for the consumption of the landed proprietors and the tillers of the soil; they were brought into general circulation, as objects of barter or as raw material. The rigid confines of the demesnial system, which had up to now hemmed in all economic activity, were broken down and the whole social order was patterned along more flexible, more active and more varied lines. As in antiquity, the country oriented itself afresh on the city. Under the influence of trade the old Roman cities took on new life and were repopulated, or mercantile groups formed round about the military burgs and established themselves along the sea coasts, on river banks, at confluences, at the junction points of the natural routes of communcation. Each of them constituted a market which exercised an attraction, proportionate to its importance, on the surrounding country or made itself felt afar.

Large or small, they were to be met everywhere; one was to be found, on the average, in every twenty-five square leagues of land. They had, in fact, become indispensable to society. They had introduced into it a division of labor which it could no longer do without. Between them and the country was established a reciprocal exchange of services. An increasingly intimate solidarity bound them together, the country attending to the provisioning of the towns, and the towns supplying, in return, articles of commerce and manufactured goods. The physical life of the burgher depended upon the peasant, but the social life of the peasant depended upon the burgher. For the burgher disclosed to him a more comfortable sort of existence, a more refined sort, and one which, in arousing his desires, multiplied his needs and raised his standard of living. And it was not only in this respect that the rise of cities strongly stimulated social progress. It made no less a contribution in spreading throughout the world a new conception of labor. Before this it had been serf; now it became free, and the consequences of this fact, to which we shall return, were incalculable. Let it be added, finally, that the economic revival of which the twelfth century saw the flowering revealed the power of capital, and enough will have been said to show that possibly no period in all history had a more profound effect upon humanity.

Invigorated, transformed and launched upon the route of progress, the new Europe resembled, in short, more the ancient Europe than the Europe of Carolingian times. For it was out of antiquity that she regained that essential characteristic of being a region of cities. And if, in the political organization, the rôle of cities had been greater in antiquity than it was in the Middle Ages, in return their economic influence in the latter era greatly exceeded what it had ever been before. Generally speaking, great mercantile cities were relatively rare in the western provinces of the Roman Empire. Aside from Rome herself, there were scarcely any at all except Naples, Milan, Marseilles and Lyons. Nothing of the sort was then in existence which might be comparable to what were, at the beginning of the tenth century, ports like Venice, Pisa, Genoa or Bruges, or centers of industry such as Milan, Florence, Ypres, and Ghent. In Gaul, in fact, the important place held in the twelfth century by ancient cities such as Orleans, Bordeaux, Cologne, Nantes, Rouen, and others, was much superior to what they had enjoyed under the emperors. Finally, the extension of the economic development of medieval Europe went well beyond the limits it had reached in Roman Europe. Instead of halting along the Rhine and the Danube, it overflowed widely in Germany and reached as far as the Vistula. Regions which had been travelled over, at the beginning of the Christian era, only by infrequent traders in amber and furs and which seemed as inhospitable as the heart of Africa might have seemed to our ancestors, now burgeoned with cities. The Sound, which no Roman trading vessel had ever crossed, was animated by the continual passage of ships. They sailed the Baltic and the North Sea as they had sailed the Mediterranean. There were almost as many ports on the shores of the one as on the shores of the other.

From two quarters, trade made use of the resources which Nature had placed at its disposal. It dominated the two inland seas which between them bounded the admirably indented coast line of the continent of Europe. Just as the Italian cities had driven back the Moslems from the Mediterranean, so in the course of the twelfth century the German cities drove back the Scandinavians from the North Sea and the Baltic, on which hereafter were spread the sails of the Hanse Towns.

Thus the commercial expansion which first made its appearance at the two points at which Europe came in contact with it—by Venice with the world of the east, by Flanders with the Russo-Scandinavian world—spread like a beneficent epidemic over the whole Continent. In reaching inland, the movement from the north and the movement from the south finally met each other. The contact between them was effected at the mid-point of the natural route which led from Bruges to Venice—on the plain of Champagne, where in the twelfth century were instituted the famous fairs of Troyes, Lagny, Provins and Bar-sur-Aube, which up to the end of the thirteenth century fulfilled, in medieval Europe, the functions of an exchange and of a clearing house.

Chapter V

THE MERCHANT CLASS

A LMOST always, in questions of origin, the amount of information available is far from satisfactory. It is therefore impossible to reconstruct an exact picture of the rise of the merchant class which inspired the commercial movement and caused it to spread over all Europe.

In certain countries, trade appears as an original and spontaneous phenomenon. This was the case, for example, at the dawn of history in Greece and Scandinavia. There, navigation was at least as old as agriculture. Everything led men to engage in it: the deep conformation of the coast-lines, the abundance of harbors, and the subtle attraction of those islands and low-lying shores which were visible on the horizon and which made a sea-faring life seem the more tempting because there was so little to be hoped for from a soil as barren as was that of the homeland. The proximity of older and poorly defended civilizations held out, in addition, the lure of rich plunder. Piracy was the initiator of maritime trade among the Greeks of the Homeric era, as among the Norse vikings; for a long time the two vocations developed in concert.

Nothing of the sort, however, was to be found in the Middle Ages. There was no sign of that heroic and barbarian occupation. The Germanic tribes that invaded the Roman provinces in the fifth century were complete strangers to a maritime life. They contented themselves with appropriating the soil, and the shipping of the Mediterranean continued, as in the past, to fill the peaceful rôle which had fallen to it under the Empire.

The Moslem invasion which caused its ruin and closed the sea provoked no reaction. The situation was taken for granted, and the continent of Europe, deprived of its traditional markets, remained an essentially rural civilization. The sporadic trade which Jews, peddlers and occasional merchants still carried on during the Carolingian era was too feeble and was too effectively discouraged by the invasions of the Norsemen and Saracens to lend support to the belief that it was the precursor of the commercial revival whose first symptoms were visible in the tenth century.

It would seem natural to suppose, at first glance, that a merchant class grew up little by little in the midst of the agricultural masses. Nothing, however, gives credence to that theory. In the social organization of the late Middle Ages, where each family from father to son was bound to the soil, it is hard to see what possibly could have induced men to exchange, for a livelihood made sure by the possession of the soil, the aleatory and precarious livelihood of the trader. The love of gain and the desire to ameliorate one's condition must have carried, at best, very little weight with a population accustomed to a traditional way of living, having no contact with the outside world, in which no novelty, no curiosity stirred the imagination, and in which the spirit of initiative was probably completely lacking. Though they frequented the small local markets the peasants never made enough money out of them to be inspired with the desire for, or even to be inclined to envisage the possibility of, a manner of life based on trade. Theirs must have seemed to them merely a normal and customary occupation. The idea of selling one's land in order to procure liquid assets certainly did not occur to any of them. The state of society and the general outlook on life was entirely opposed to it. There is not the slightest proof that anybody had ever dreamed of a transaction so bizarre and so hazardous.

Certain historians have sought to set up as the forerunners of the merchants of the Middle Ages those servitors whom the great abbeys charged with procuring, from without, the indispensable commodities for their subsistence and to whom they sometimes entrusted the selling, in the neighboring markets, of the surplus of their own harvests and vintages. This hypothesis, ingenious as it is, does not stand up under examination. In the first place, the "abbey-merchants" were too few in number to have an influence of any great moment. In the second place, they were not free agents, but employees exclusively in the service of their masters. It is not apparent that any of them ever carried on business on his own account. No attempt has been successful, and none, certainly, ever will be successful, to establish a connecting link between them and the merchant class whose origins we are looking for here.

All that can be asserted with certainty is that the commercial *profession* appeared in Venice at a period when nothing yet gave reason to expect its spread in Western Europe. Cassiodorus, in the sixth century, describes the Venetians as even then a sailor- and merchant-folk. It is an established fact that in the ninth century some very great fortunes were founded in the city. The treaties of commerce which Venice later concluded with the Carolingian emperors or with those of Byzantium, furthermore, leave no room for doubt as to the nature of the life of her inhabitants. Unfortunately there are no existing data on the manner in which their capital was accumulated and their business carried on. It is more than probable that salt, prepared on the islets of the lagoons, formed at an early date the substance of a lucrative export trade. The coastal trade along the shores of the Adriatic and especially the relations of the city with Constantinople resulted in still greater profits. The extent to which the technique of Venetian commerce had already been perfected by the tenth century is extraordinary.

At a period when everywhere else in Europe instruction was the exclusive monopoly of the clergy, the ability to write was widespread in Venice. It is perfectly obvious that there was a close relation between this curious phenomenon and the development of trade.

It was the credit system, which, with the greatest probability, helped commerce to reach at an early date the point it had attained. To be sure, there are no records bearing on the matter, earlier than the first part of the eleventh century. But the custom of maritime loans seems to have already been so highly developed at this period that their origin must necessarily be dated much earlier.

The Venetian merchant was in the habit of borrowing from a capitalist the money necessary for financing a cargo, at a rate of interest which averaged in general about twenty per cent. A ship was loaded by several merchants acting in common, and the perils of navigation led maritime expeditions to be made up of flotillas comprising several vessels manned by large and carefully armed crews. Everything tends to show that the profits were extremely high. If, in this respect, Venetian documents hardly give precise information, we can compensate for their silence by means of Genoese sources. In the twelfth century maritime loans, the equipments of ships, and business methods were alike in both cities. What we know about the enormous profits realized by Genoese mariners must then hold equally true for their precursors of Venice. And we know enough about it to be able to state that trade and trade alone, in the one quarter as in the other, could have enabled those, whose fortunes were favored by energy and intelligence, to acquire abundant capital.

But the secret of the rapid and early fortunes of the Venetian merchants is undoubtedly to be found in the close relationship which bound their commercial organization to that of Byzantium, and through Byzantium to the commercial organization of antiquity. In reality Venice belonged to the west only by her geographical location; in the life that animated her and the spirit that inspired her, she was foreign to it. The first colonists of the lagoons, fugitives from Aquileia and neighboring cities, brought there the economic technique and tools of the Roman world. The constant and increasingly active relations which, from then on, continued to bind the city to Byzantine Italy and Constantinople, protected and developed that important commercial center. In short, between Venice and the east, where was preserved the thousand-year-old tradition of civilization, contact was never lost. Venetian navigators may be considered as the successor of those Syrian mariners who were so active, up to the time of the Moslem invasion, in the port of Marseilles and the Tyrrhenian Sea. They had no need of a long and painful apprenticeship to fit them for a great commerce. The tradition of it had, with them, never been lost, and that is enough to explain the peculiar place they occupy in the economic history of Western Europe. It is impossible to deny that the commercial law and customs of antiquity were the cause of the superiority which they manifested and which they enjoyed from the very start. Thorough research will, some day, doubtless supply definite proof of what is here merely asserted. There is no doubt, meanwhile, but that the Byzantine influence, so characteristic of the political constitution of Venice during the early centuries, had also impregnated its economic constitution. In the rest of Europe the commercial profession was tardily evolved from a civilization in which every former trace of it had long since been lost. In Venice it appeared at the same time as the city itself; there it was a survival from the Roman world.

Venice naturally exercised a profound effect upon the other maritime cities which, in the course of the eleventh century, commenced to appear: Pisa and Genoa first, later Marseilles and Barcelona. But she does not seem to have contributed to the formation of the merchant class by virtue of which commercial activity spread little by little from the shores of the sea towards the interior of the Continent. Here we find ourselves in the presence of a quite different phenomenon, one which there are no grounds for believing was connected with the economic organization of antiquity. To be sure, Venetian merchants were to be met with at an early date not only in Lombardy but even north of the Alps. But it is not apparent that they founded colonies anywhere. The conditions underlying commerce on the land were, after all, too different from those of commerce on the sea to make it likely that they had an influence. There are, furthermore, no existing records to that effect.

It was in the course of the tenth century that there reappeared in continental Europe a class of professional merchants whose progress, very slow at first, gathered speed as the following century moved forward. The increase in population, which began to be manifest at the same era, is certainly in direct relation to this phenomenon. It had as a result the detaching from the land an increasingly important number of individuals and committing them to that roving and hazardous existence which, in every agricultural civilization, is the lot of those who no longer find themselves with their roots in the soil. It multiplied the crowd of vagabonds drifting about all through society, living from day to day by alms from the monasteries, hiring themselves out at harvest-time, enlisting in the armies in time of war and holding back from neither rapine nor pillage when occasion presented. It is among this crowd of foot-loose adventurers that the first adepts of trade must, without any doubt, be looked for.

Their manner of life naturally drove them towards all those localities where the affluence of the inhabitants gave them the hope of gain or offered some fortunate opening. If they assiduously took part in pilgrimages, they were certainly no less drawn by the ports, the markets, and the fairs. There they hired themselves out as sailors,

as boatmen, as stevedores or porters. Energetic
characters, tempered by the experience of a life
full of the unexpected, must have abounded
among them. Many knew foreign languages and
were conversant with the customs and needs of
divers lands. Let a lucky chance present itself—
and heaven knows that chances are numerous in
the life of a vagabond—they were remarkably
well equipped to profit thereby. And a small profit,
with skill and intelligence, can always be turned
into a big profit. This must have been particularly true in an era when the insufficiency of communications and the relative rarity of merchandise offered for sale must have naturally kept
prices at a very high level. Famines were multiplied throughout Europe, sometimes in one province and sometimes in another, by that inadequate
system of communications, and increased still
more the opportunities, for those who knew how
to make use of them, of getting rich. A few timely
sacks of wheat, transported to the right spot, sufficed for the realizing of huge profits. For a man,
adroit and sparing no pains, Fortune then held
out the prospect of fruitful operations. It was
certainly not long before nouveaux riches made
their appearance in the midst of this miserable
crowd of impoverished, bare-foot wanderers in
the world.

Fortunately there happen to be sources of information which supply proof that this was in fact the case. It will suffice to cite here the most characteristic of them, the biography of St. Godric of Finchale.

He was born towards the end of the eleventh century in Lincolnshire, of poor peasant stock, and he must have been put to it from early childhood to find a means of livelihood. Like many other unfortunates in every age, he was a beachcomber, on the lookout for wreckage cast up by the waves. Next, perhaps following some lucky find, he played the rôle of peddler and went about the country with a pack on his back. Eventually he accumulated a little capital and, one fine day, he joined a band of merchants met in the course of his peregrinations. With them he went from market to market, from fair to fair, from town to town. Thus become a merchant by profession, he rapidly realized profits big enough to enable him to form an association with his fellows, to load a ship in common with them and to engage in coastal trade along the shores of England, Scotland, Denmark and Flanders. The company prospered to the fullest. Its operations consisted in shipping abroad goods which were known to be scarce, and there picking up in return merchandise which it took care to dispose of in places where the demand was the greatest and where might be realized, in consequence, the largest profits. At the end of several years this prudent custom of buying cheap and selling dear made of Godric a very rich man. It was then that, moved by grace, he suddenly renounced the life he had led until then, turned over his possessions to the poor, and became a hermit.

The story of St. Godric, if we eliminate from it the mystic ending, was that of a great many others. It shows, with the utmost clearness, how a man, starting with nothing, was able in a relatively short time to amass considerable money. Circumstances and luck probably contributed largely to the making of his fortune. But the essential cause of his success, and the contemporary biography to which we owe the account lays abundant stress thereon, was intelligence, or rather business sense.[1] Godric seems to have been a shrewd calculator gifted with that commercial instinct which it is not altogether rare to meet, in any age, among enter-

[1] "*Sic itaque puerilibus annis simpliciter domi transactis, caepit adolescentior prudentiores vitae vias excolere et documenta secularis providentiae sollicite et exercitate perdicere.* Unde non agriculturae delegit exercitia colere, sed potius quae sagacioris animi sunt rudimenta studuit, arripiendo exercere. *Hinc est quod mercatoris aemulatus studium, coepit mercimonii frequentare negotium, et primitus in minoribus quidem et rebus pretii inferioris, coepit lucrandi officia discere; postmodum vero paulatim ad majoris pretii emolumenta adolescentiae suae ingenia promovere."* Libellus de Vita S. Godrici, p. 25.

prising natures. The quest of profit guided all his actions and in him can be easily recognized that famous "capitalistic spirit" (*spiritus capitalisticus*) which some would have us believe dates only from the Renaissance. It is preposterous to submit that Godric carried on his business merely to provide for his daily needs. In place of hoarding in the bottom of some chest the money he gained, he used it only to maintain and extend his trading. It is not employing too modern an expression to say that the profits he realized were put to work as fast as possible to augment his revolving capital. For that matter, it is somewhat surprising to observe that the conscience of this future monk was completely free of all religious scruple. His zeal in searching out for every commodity the market where it would produce the maximum profit was in flagrant opposition to the disapproval with which the Church looked upon every kind of speculation, and to the economic doctrine of "fair price."

The fortune of Godric is not to be explained merely by business ability. In a society still as crude as that of the eleventh century, private initiative could succeed only by having recourse to cooperation. Too many perils threatened the wandering existence of the merchant not to impose on him first of all the fundamental necessity of forming in groups for the sake of common defense. Still other motives impelled him to unite with his fellows. At fairs and markets, should a dispute arise, he found in them favorable witnesses, or bondsmen who would be security for him in a court of justice. In common with them he was able to buy at wholesale merchandise which, left to his own resources, he would have been unable to get. His credit was increased by the collective credit of which he supplied a part, and thanks thereto he was able more easily to come out on top in competition with his rivals. The biography of Godric informs us in its own very words that from the day when its hero associated himself with a band of merchants his fortunes took their upward turn. In taking this step he merely conformed to custom. Trade in the late Middle Ages was known only in that primitive form of which the caravan is the characteristic manifestation. Maritime or land trade was possible only by grace of the mutual assurance an association inspired in its members, of the discipline which it imposed upon them, of the regulations to which it subjected them. And this feature was always in evidence. Boats sailed only when assembled in flotillas, just as merchants travelled the country only in bands. Security existed for them only if guaranteed by force, and force was an attribute of collectivity.

It would be a complete mistake to see in the merchant associations, of which traces may be found in the tenth century, a peculiarly German phenomenon. It is true that the terms which were used to designate them in the north of Europe—*gild* and *hanse*—came originally from Germany. But this habit of cooperating is to be found everywhere in economic life and, whatever may have been the differences in the details, in what was essential it was everywhere the same, because everywhere there were the same conditions which made it indispensable. In Italy as in the Netherlands, trade was able to expand only by cooperation. The *frairies,* the *charités,* the merchant *compagnies* of the countries of the Roman tongue were exactly analogous to the *gilds* and *hanses* of the German territories.[2] What determined the economic organization was not "national genius," but social necessity. The primitive institutions of trade were as cosmopolitan as those of the feudal system.

The sources of information make it possible to obtain an excellent idea of the merchant troops which, beginning with the tenth century, were to be found in greater and greater numbers in West-

[2] We even find a similar organization in Dalmatia. See C. Jirecek, "Die Bedeutung von Raguza in der Handelsgeschichte des Mittelalters," *Almanak der Akademie der Wissenschaften, in Wien,* 1899, p. 382.

ern Europe. They should be pictured as armed bands, the members of which, equipped with bows and swords, encircled the horses and wagons loaded with bags, packs and casks. At the head of the caravan marched a standard-bearer. A chief, the *Hansgraf* or the *Doyen*, exercised his authority over the company. This latter was composed of "brothers," bound together by an oath of fidelity. A spirit of close solidarity animated the whole group. The merchandise, apparently, was bought and sold in common and the profits divided pro rata, according to the share of each one in the association.

It seems that these companies, as a general rule, made very long journeys. It would be a decided mistake to conceive of the commerce of this era as a local commerce, strictly confined within the orbit of a regional market. It has already been seen that Italian traders went as far as Paris and Flanders. At the end of the tenth century the port of London was regularly frequented by merchants from Cologne, Huy, Dinant, Flanders and Rouen. A contemporary text speaks of men from Verdun trading with Spain. In the valley of the Seine, the Parisian hanse of river merchants was in constant relations with Rouen. The biography of Godric, in chronicling his distant expeditions in the Baltic and the North Sea, at the same time throws light on those of his fellows.

It was therefore trade on a big scale or, if you prefer a more precise term, trade over long distances, that was characteristic of the economic revival of the Middle Ages. Just as the shipping of Venice and Amalfi and later that of Pisa and Genoa launched forth from the very beginning on long sea voyages, so did the merchants of the Continent lead their vagabond life over wide territories. It is quite clear that this was for them the sole means of realizing big profits. To get high prices it was necessary to seek afar the products which were there found in abundance, in order to be able to resell them later at a profit in places where their rarity increased their value. The more distant the journey of the merchant, the more profitable was it for him. And it is easily appreciated how the desire for gain was strong enough to counterbalance the hardships, the risks and the dangers of a wandering existence open to every hazard. Except during the winter, the merchant of the Middle Ages was continually on the road. English texts of the twelfth century picturesquely designated him under the name of *piepowdrous*— "dusty-foot."

This rover, this vagabond of trade, by the strangeness of his manner of life must have, from the very first, astonished the agricultural society to all of the customs of which he went counter and in which no place was set aside for him. He brought mobility to the midst of people attached to the soil; he revealed, to a world faithful to tradition.and respectful of a hierarchy which fixed the rôle and the rank of each class, a shrewd and rationalist activity in which fortune, instead of being measured by social status, depended only on intelligence and energy. And so it is not surprising that he gave offense. The nobility never had anything but disdain for these upstarts come from no one knew where, and whose insolent good fortune they could not bear. They were infuriated to see them better supplied with money than themselves; they were humiliated by being obliged to have recourse, in time of trouble, to the purse of these newly rich. Save in Italy, where aristocratic families did not hesitate to augment their fortunes by having an interest in commercial operations in the capacity of money-lender, the prejudice that it was degrading to engage in business remained deep-rooted in the heart of the feudal caste up to the time of the French Revolution.

As to the clergy, their attitude in regard to merchants was still more unfavorable. In the eyes of the Church, commercial life was dangerous to the safety of the soul. "The merchant," says a text at-

tributed to St. Jerome "can please God only with
difficulty." Trade seemed to the canonists to be
a form of usury. They condemned profit-seeking,
which they confounded with avarice. Their doctrine of "fair price" was meant to impose a re-
nouncement of economic life and, in short, an
asceticism incompatible with the natural development of the latter. Every form of speculation
seemed to them a sin. And this severity was not
entirely caused by the strict interpretation of Christian morality. Very likely, it should also be attributed to the conditions under which the Church
existed. The subsistence of the Church, in fact, depended exclusively on that demesnial organization
which, as has been seen above, was so foreign to
the idea of enterprise and profit. If to this be
added the ideal of poverty which Clunisian mysticism gave to religious fervor, it can be readily
understood why the Church took a defiant and
hostile attitude toward the commercial revival
which must, from the very first, have seemed to it
a thing of shame and a cause of anxiety.[3]

We must admit, however, that this attitude was
not without its benefits. It certainly resulted in
preventing the passion for gain from spreading

[3] "The Life of Saint Guidon of Anderlecht," *Acta Sanctorum*,
Vol. IV, p. 42, speaks of the *"ignobilis mercatura"* and calls a
merchant who advised the saint to apply himself to it a *"diaboli
minister."*

without limit; it protected, in a certain measure, the poor from the rich, debtors from creditors. The scourge of debts, which in Greek and Roman antiquity so sorely afflicted the people, was spared the social order of the Middle Ages, and it may well be that the Church contributed largely to that happy result. The universal prestige it enjoyed served as a moral check-rein. If it was not strong enough to subject the traders to the doctrine of "fair price," it was strong enough to restrain them from giving way entirely to greediness for profits. They were certainly very uneasy over the peril to which their way of living exposed their eternal salvation. The fear of the future life tormented their conscience. Many there were who, on their death beds, founded by their wills charitable institutions or appropriated a part of their wealth to reimburse sums unjustly acquired. The edifying end of Godric testifies to the inner conflict which must often have been waged in their souls, torn between the irresistible seductions of wealth and the austere prescriptions of religious morality which their profession obliged them, in spite of their veneration, to violate unceasingly.[4]

[4] An example of the conversion of a merchant quite analogous to that of Godric and at the same epoch is given by the "Vita Theogeri," *Monumenta Germaniae historica*, Vol. XII, p. 457.

The legal status of the merchants eventually gave them a thoroughly singular place in that society which they astonished in so many respects. By virtue of the wandering existence they led, they were everywhere regarded as foreigners. No one knew the origins of these eternal travellers. Certainly the majority among them were born of non-free parents, from whom they had early taken leave in order to launch upon adventures. But serfdom was not to be presumed: it had to be proven. The law necessarily treated as a free man one who could not be ascribed to a master. It therefore came about that it was necessary to treat the merchants, most of whom were without doubt the sons of serfs, as if they had always enjoyed freedom. In detaching themselves from their natal soil they had freed themselves in fact. In the midst of a social organization where the populace was attached to the land and where everyone was dependent upon a liege lord, they presented the strange picture of circulating everywhere without being claimed by anyone. They did not demand freedom; it was conceded to them because no one could prove that they did not already enjoy it. They acquired it, so to speak, by usage and limitation. In short, just as agrarian civilization had made of the peasant a man whose normal state was servitude, trade made of the merchant a man whose normal condition was liberty. From that time on, in place of being subject to seignorial and demesnial jurisdiction, he was answerable only to public jurisdiction. Alone competent to try him were the tribunals which still kept, above the multitude of private courts, the old framework of the judicial constitution of the Frankish State.

Public authority at the same time took him under its protection. The local princes whose task it was to preserve, in their territories, peace and public order—to which pertained the policing of the highways and the safeguarding of travellers— extended their tutelage over the merchants. In doing so they did nothing more than to continue the tradition of the State, the powers of which they had usurped. In that agricultural empire of his, Charlemagne himself had given careful attention to the maintenance of the freedom of circulation. He had issued edicts in favor of pilgrims and traders, Jew or Christian, and the capitularies of his successors attest to the fact that they remained faithful to that policy. The emperors of the House of Saxony followed suit in Germany, and the kings of France, after they came into power, did likewise. The princes had, furthermore, every interest in attracting numerous merchants to their countries, whither they brought a new animation and where they augmented bountifully the revenues from the market-tolls. The counts early took active measures against highwaymen, watching over the good conduct of the fairs and the security of the routes of communication. In the eleventh century great progress had been made and the chroniclers state that there were regions where one could travel with a sack full of gold without running the risk of being despoiled. On its part, the Church punished highwaymen with excommunication, and the Truces of God, in which it took the initiative in the tenth century, protected the merchants in particular.

But it was not enough that merchants be placed under the safeguard and the jurisdiction of the public authority. The novelty of their profession had further consequences. It forced a law, made for a civilization based on agriculture, to become more flexible and to adapt itself to the fundamental needs which this novelty imposed upon it. Judicial procedure, with its rigid and traditional formalism, with its delays, with its methods of proof as primitive as the duel, with its abuse of the absolutory oath, with its "ordeals" which left to chance the outcome of a trial, was for the merchants a perpetual nuisance. They needed a simpler legal system, more expeditious and more equitable. At the fairs and markets they elaborated among themselves a commercial code (*jus mercatorum*) of which the oldest traces may be noted by the beginning of the eleventh century. Most probably it was introduced very early into the legal practice, at least for suits between merchants. It must have constituted for them a sort of personal law, the benefits of which the judges had no motive for refusing them. The contemporary texts which make allusion to it unfortunately do not make clear its terms. There is, however, no doubt but that it was a collection of usages born of business experience and which spread from place to place commensurately with the spread of trade itself. The great fairs whither came, periodically, merchants from divers countries and which had a special tribunal charged with the rendering of speedy justice, must have seen from the very first the elaboration of a sort of commercial jurisprudence, the same everywhere despite the differences in country, language, and national laws.

The merchant thus seems to have been not only a free man but a privileged man to boot. Like the cleric and the noble, he enjoyed a law of exception. Like them, he escaped the demesnial and seignorial authority which continued to bear down upon the peasants.

Chapter VI

THE MIDDLE CLASS

IN no civilization is city life evolved independently of commerce and industry. Neither antiquity nor modern times show any exception to
this rule. Diversity of climates, peoples or relig-
ions is as immaterial as diversity of eras. It is a
rule which held true, in the past, in the cities of
Egypt, Babylonia, Greece, and the Roman and
Arab Empires, just as in our day it has held true
in the cities of Europe, America, India, Japan,
and China.

Its universality is explained by exigence. A city
group, in fact, can live only by importing its food-
supply from outside. But with this importation
must correspond, on the other hand, an exportation of manufactured products constituting a
counterpart or countervalue. Thus is established,
between the city and the surrounding country, a
close interrelation of services. Commerce and industry are indispensable to the maintenance of
this reciprocal dependence; without the first, to
assure a steady traffic, without the second, to fur-

nish goods for exchange, the city would perish.[1]

This condition is obviously subject to any quantity of variations. Depending on time and place, sometimes commercial activity and sometimes industrial activity is the dominant characteristic of a city population. In antiquity, of course, a considerable section of the city population was made up of landed proprietors, living either by the cultivation of or by the revenue from the lands which they owned outside. But it remains none the less true that commensurately with the development of cities, artisans and traders became more and more numerous. The rural economy, older than the urban economy, continued to exist side by side with the latter; the one did not prevent the other from developing.

The cities of the Middle Ages present a very different picture. Commerce and industry made them what they were. They did not cease to grow under that influence. At no era in history is there so marked a contrast as that which their social and economic organization presented to the social and economic organization of the country. Never be-

[1] This is true, naturally, only for towns placed under normal conditions. The State has often had to maintain city populations much too numerous to be able to take care of their own subsistence. This, for example, had been the case with Rome since the end of the Republic. But the increase of the population in Rome was the result of political, not economic, causes.

fore had there existed, it seems, a class of men so
specifically and strictly urban as was the medieval
bourgeoisie.[2]

That the origin of these cities is directly related,
as an effect to its cause, to the commercial revival
of which we have spoken in the preceding chapters, it is impossible to doubt. The proof is to be
found in the striking correspondence which is to
be noted between the expansion of trade and the
rise of cities. Italy and the Netherlands, where
commerce first showed itself, are precisely the
countries where cities made their first appearance
and where they developed most rapidly and vigor-
ously. It is easy to mark how, in step with the
progress of trade, towns multiplied. They appeared along all the natural routes by which trade
spread. They were born, so to speak, under its
footsteps. They are found, at first, only along sea
coasts and rivers. Then, as the commercial pene-
tration spread, others were founded along the
transverse roads which connected these first centers of activity with each other.

[2] There were certainly in the Middle Ages numbers of localities
bearing the title "city" and endowed with city franchises, of
which the inhabitants were much more occupied with agriculture
than with commerce or industry. But in this case they were the
product of a later era. We are alluding here to the middle class
as it was first constituted and as it continued to exist in the
characteristic centers of city life.

The case of the Netherlands is quite typical. In the tenth century the earlier towns were founded on the shore of the sea or on the banks of the Meuse and the Scheldt; the intermediate region, Brabant, did not yet know them. We must wait until the twelfth century before they make their appearance on the route which lay between those two great rivers. Similar observations may be made anywhere. A map of Europe on which was marked the relative importance of the commercial highways would coincide very closely with an abstract of the relative importance of the city groups.

The towns of the Middle Ages showed an extraordinary diversity. Each had a distinctive physiognomy and particular characteristics. Every one of them differed from the others just as men differ among themselves. They can, however, be classified according to certain general types. And these types themselves resemble one another in their essential traits. It is therefore not a hopeless task to try to depict, as we shall endeavor to do here, the evolution of city life in the west of Europe. Doubtless the picture will necessarily be a little too schematic, not fitting exactly any one particular case but rather being the description of what is common to a whole species, an abstract of individual characteristics. Only the general outlines will appear, as in a landscape viewed from a mountain top.

The subject, however, is less complicated than would appear at first glance. It is futile, indeed, in an outline of the origin of European cities, to take count of the infinite complexity which they manifested. City life was developed first of all in only a quite restricted number of localities in Northern Italy, in the Netherlands, and in neighboring regions. It will be enough if we confine ourselves to these latter, neglecting the later developments which, whatever might be of interest in them, were actually only duplicate phenomena.[3] Yet in the following pages a privileged place will be accorded to the Netherlands. This is because that country supplies the historian with more abundant illumination on the early days of city evolution than any other region of Western Europe.

The organization of commerce in the Middle Ages, as it has been described in the preceding chapter, obliged the peripatetic merchants or "merchant adventurers," on whom it relied, to settle at fixed points. In the interval between their

[3] The most important towns for the study of the origins of city institutions are evidently the oldest; it is there that the middle class arose. It is a faulty method to seek to explain the latter by relying on towns of later and tardy development, such as those of Germany beyond the Rhine.

trips and especially during the bad season which made the sea, the rivers and the roads impassable, they necessarily had to gather at certain places in the region. It was naturally in localities of which the site, by its facilities in the matter of communications, lent itself best to the exigencies of trade and where they could at the same time place their money and goods in security, that the merchants established their residence. They therefore repaired to the towns and burgs which best met these conditions.

The number of them was considerable. The site of the towns had been determined by the conformation of the terrain or the direction of the river courses—in short, by conditions of nature, which were precisely what determined the direction of trade and so steered the merchants towards them. In the same way the burgs, which had been designed to resist enemies or furnish a shelter to the population, were naturally built in localities particularly easy of access. It was by the same routes the invaders passed that the merchants travelled, and the result was that fortresses erected against the former were excellently situated for attracting the latter to their walls. Thus it came about that the first commercial groups were formed in neighborhoods which Nature had pre-

disposed to become—or to become again—the focal points of economic circulation.

There are apparent grounds for belief, and certain historians have in fact believed, that these
first agglomerations were due to the markets established in such great number, beginning with
the ninth century. Inviting as it seems at first
glance, this opinion does not bear scrutiny. The
markets of the Carolingian era were simple local
markets, frequented by peasants from roundabout, and by a few peddlers. They had as their
sole aim the provisioning of the towns and burgs.
They were not held more than once a week and
their operations were limited by the household
needs of the inhabitants, very few in number, for
whose benefit they had been instituted. Markets
of this sort have always existed and still exist in
our own day in thousands of little towns and villages. Their attraction was not strong enough nor
widespread enough to draw and hold a mercantile
population. We know, moreover, of any number
of places which, although equipped with markets
of this sort, never rose to the rank of cities.
Such, for example, was the case with those which
the Bishop of Cambrai and the Abbot of Reich-
enau established, the one in 1001 at Le Câteau-
Cambrésis and the other in 1100 at Radolfzell. Yet
Le Câteau and Radolfzell never were anything but

insignificant localities from an economic viewpoint, and the failure of the attempts of which
they were the object clearly shows that markets of
this sort were wanting in that influence which one
is sometimes minded to accord them.

As much might be said of the fairs (*fora*), and
yet the fairs in contrast to the markets do not show
a strictly local character; they were instituted to
serve as a periodic meeting place for the professional merchants, to put them in touch with each
other, and to get them to gather there at fixed sea-
sons. In fact, the importance of many of these
fairs was very great. In Flanders those of
Thourout and Messines and in France those of
Bar-sur-Aube and Lagny figured among the principal centers of medieval trade up to near the end
of the twelfth century. It may therefore seem
strange that none of these localities became a city
worthy of the name. This is because whatever
activity they showed was lacking in that permanent character which is necessary for the fixation
of trade. Merchants directed their steps toward
them because they were situated on the great route
of travel running from the North Sea to Lombardy, and because they enjoyed special franchises and privileges there. They were points of
assembly and places of exchange where buyers
and sellers from the north and south were to be

encountered. After a few weeks their exotic clientèle dispersed, not to return before the following year.

It probably happened—and it very often did happen, as a matter of fact—that a fair was located at the spot where already existed a mercantile group. The one may have assisted the development of the other. But it is impossible to hold that this was the real cause of its existence. Several great cities can be named, which never had a privileged market or which did not have one until very late. Worms, Speyer, or Mainz never was the seat of a fair; Tournai had one only in 1284, Leyden in 1304, and Ghent in the fifteenth century only. The fact therefore remains that geographical advantages plus the presence of a town or a fortified burg seems the essential and necessary condition for a colony of merchants.

Nothing is less artificial than the development of a colony of this sort. The fundamental needs of commerce—ease of communication and security—account for it in the most natural way. In a more advanced era, when better methods would permit man to conquer Nature and to force his presence upon her despite handicaps of climate or of soil, it would doubtless have been possible to build towns anywhere the spirit of enterprise and the quest of gain might suggest a site. But it was quite another matter in a period when society had not yet acquired enough vigor to rise above the physical conditions in the midst of which it developed. It naturally adapted itself to them and in accordance with them its life was regulated. In short, the towns of the Middle Ages were a phenomenon determined as much by physical surroundings as the course of rivers is determined by the conformation of the mountains and the direction of the valleys.

As the commercial revival in Europe gained headway after the tenth century, the merchant colonies established in the towns or at the foot of the burgs enjoyed an uninterrupted growth. Their population increased through the action of economic vitality. Up to the end of the thirteenth century, the progress which had been manifest from the start continued steadily. No other course was open. Each of the focal points of international traffic naturally shared in this activity, and the multiplication of merchants naturally resulted in an increase of their number in all the spots where they had first settled, for these spots were exactly the ones most favorable to commercial life. If they had attracted the traders sooner than others did, it is because they, better than the others, satisfied their professional requirements. Here, therefore, is a thoroughly satisfactory explanation of the fact that, as a general rule, the greatest commercial cities in a region were also the oldest.

There is by no means enough information to satisfy our curiosity concerning these primitive mercantile groups. The historiography of the tenth and eleventh centuries is completely unconcerned with social and economic phenomena. Written exclusively by clerics or by monks, it naturally measured the importance and the value of events according to how they affected the Church. Lay society did not claim their attention save in so far as it related to religious society. They could not neglect the recital of the wars and political conflicts which reacted on the Church, but there was no reason for them to have taken pains to note the beginnings of city life, for which they were lacking in comprehension no less than in sympathy.[4] A few allusions made incidentally, a few fragmentary annotations upon the occasion of a disorder or an uprising—this is what the historian is obliged to content himself with. We must go to the twelfth century to get, here and there from some rare layman dabbling in writing, a little more substantial prize. Maps and

---

[4] The chronicler Gilles d'Orval, for example, speaking of the franchises granted the town of Huy by the Bishop of Liège in 1066, mentions a few points and passes over the rest in silence "in order not to bore the reader." He is evidently thinking of the ecclesiastical public for which he is writing.

records supplement this poverty to a certain extent. Yet they are rare indeed for the period of origins. It is only by the end of the eleventh century that they begin to throw a little more abundant illumination. As for first-hand sources—that is to say, written and compiled by townsmen— none exist earlier than the end of the twelfth century. It is therefore necessary, although there are a few, to ignore them and to have recourse, too often, to inference and hypothesis in this study of origins.

Details are lacking concerning the gradual peopling of the towns. It is not known how the first traders, who came to locate there, settled in the midst of the pre-existing population. The towns, whose precincts frequently included unoccupied areas given over to fields and gardens, must have furnished them at the start with a place which soon became too restricted. It is certain that in many of them, from the tenth century on, they were forced to locate outside the walls. At Verdun they built a fortified enclosure (*negotiatorum claustrum*), joined to the city by two bridges. At Ratisbonne the "city of merchants" (*urbs mercatorum*) arose beside the episcopal city, and the same thing is to be seen at Strasbourg and elsewhere.[5] At Cambrai the newcomers surrounded

[5] In the old municipal laws of Strasbourg, the new agglomeration is called *"urbs exterior."*

themselves with a palisade of wood which a little later was replaced by a stone rampart. At Marseilles the circuit of the city must have been enlarged at the beginning of the eleventh century. It would be easy to multiply these examples. They establish beyond question the rapid extensions undergone by the old cities which had not hitherto witnessed any growth since the Roman era.

The peopling of the burgs was due to the same causes as that of the towns, but it worked out under quite different conditions. Here, in fact, available space was not to be had by the new arrivals. The burgs were merely fortresses whose walls enclosed a strictly limited area. The result was that, at the start, the merchants were driven to settle outside this area because there was no other place for them. They built beside the burgs an "outside burg"—that is to say, a "faubourg" (*forisburgus, suburbium*). This suburb was called, by contemporary texts, the "new burg" (*novus burgus*), in contrast to the feudal burg or "old burg" (*vetus burgus*) to which it was joined. In the Netherlands and in England there was a word used to designate it which corresponded admirably to its nature—*portus*.

In the administrative terminology of the Roman Empire, not a sea port, but an enclosed place serving as storehouse or transfer point for merchandise was called a *portus*. The expression was passed on, with hardly any change, to the Merovingian and Carolingian eras. It is obvious that all the places to which it was applied were situated on watercourses and that market-tolls were collected in them. They were, therefore, landing places where was accumulated in the natural course of trading operations merchandise destined to be shipped further.[6]

Between a *portus* and a market or a fair the distinction is very clear. While the latter were periodic meeting places of buyers and sellers, the former was a permanent place of trade, a center of uninterrupted traffic. After the seventh century Dinant, Huy, Valenciennes and Cambrai were places with a *portus*, and in consequence transfer points. The economic slump of the eighth century and the Norseman invasions naturally ruined their business. It was not until the tenth century that the old *portus* took on new life or new ones were established, as at Bruges, Ghent, Ypres, St. Omer, and elsewhere. At the same date there appears in Anglo-Saxon texts the word "port," employed as a synonym for the Latin words *urbs* and *civitas*, and even at the present day the term

[6] In the twelfth century the word still retained its original meaning of landing place: *"Infra burgum Brisach et Argentinensem civitatem, nullus erit portus,* qui vulgo dicitur Ladstadt, *nisi apud Brisach,"* H. G. Gengler, *Stadtrechtsaltertümer,* p. 44.

"port" is commonly met with in the names of
cities of every land of English speech.

Nothing shows more clearly the close connection that existed between the economic revival of
the Middle Ages and the beginnings of city life.
They were so intimately related that the same
word which designated a commercial settlement
served in one of the great idioms of Europe to
designate the town itself. Old Dutch supplies a
similar instance. In it the word *poort* and the
word *poorter* are both employed, the first with the
meaning of "town" and the second with that of
"townsman."

It can be definitely assumed that the *portus*, so
frequently spoken of during the tenth and eleventh centuries, at the foot of the burgs of Flanders
and contiguous regions, were made up of merchant groups. Several passages in the chronicles
or lives of the saints which deal with the subject,
though in scant detail, leave no room for doubt
on this point. It will be enough to cite here the
curious narrative of the *Miracula St. Womari*,
written about 1060 by a monk who was an eye-
witness of the events he reported. Here we have
to do with a band of monks arriving in proces-
sion at Ghent. The inhabitants go out to meet
them, "like a swarm of bees." They conduct their

pious visitors first to the Church of St. Pharaïlde, situated within the limits of the burg. The next day they leave the latter to repair to the Church of St. John the Baptist, recently erected in the *portus*. It therefore seems that here is a case of the juxtaposition of two residential centers of different origin and nature. The one, the older, is a fortress and the other, the more recent, is a place of trade, and it is from the gradual fusion of these two elements, of which the first is absorbed little by little by the second, that the city is born.

It will be well to take note, before going further, of the fate of those towns and burgs whose location did not favor their becoming commercial centers. Typical examples, without going outside the Netherlands, were Térouanne or the burgs built about the monasteries of Stavelot, Malmédy, Lobbes, etc. In the agricultural and demesnial civilization of the Middle Ages, all these places were notable for their wealth and their influence. But, situated too far from the great highways of communication, they were not affected by the economic revival nor, so to speak, fecundated thereby. In the midst of the flowering which it inspired, they remained sterile, like seed fallen upon stony ground. None of them rose above the rank of

mere half-rural market-towns.[7] And it is not to
the point, furthermore, to show that in the evolution of the city, the towns and the burgs had on
the whole only an auxiliary function. Adapted to
a social order very different from that which witnessed the birth of cities, they could not have been
able to create the latter out of their own resources.
They were, so to speak, the crystallization points of
commercial activity. This did not originate in them
—it came to them from without, when favorable
conditions of site brought it their way. Their rôle
was essentially a passive rôle. In the history of
the development of cities, the commercial suburb
was considerably more important than the feudal
burg. It was the suburb that was the active element, and, as will be seen later, therein lies the
explanation of that renewal of municipal life
which was merely the consequence of the economic
revival.[8]

[7] We may make the same observation concerning the towns of
Bavai and Tongres, which had been important administrative
centers in the North of Gaul during the Roman era. Not being
situated on any watercourse, they did not profit by the commercial revival. Bavai disappeared in the ninth century; Tongres
has remained without any importance up to our own day.

[8] Naturally, no claim is made that the evolution took place in
exactly the same way in every city. The merchant suburb is not
everywhere so clearly distinguished from the original burg as
it is, for instance, in Flemish cities. According to local conditions,
the immigrant merchants and artisans formed their colonies in
divers ways. Here merely the main outlines of the subject can
be indicated.

A striking characteristic of the merchant groups was their uninterrupted growth, beginning with the tenth century. Therein they show the most violent contrast to the immobility in which the towns and the burgs, at the feet of which they were located, persisted. They continually drew to themselves new inhabitants. They expanded steadily, covering a larger and larger area, so much so that in many places they had, by the start of the twelfth century, already surrounded on all sides the original fortresses about which their houses pressed. After the beginning of the twelfth century, it became necessary to create new parishes for them. At Ghent, at Bruges, at St. Omer, and in many other places, contemporary texts remark the construction of these churches, due often to the initiative of wealthy merchants.[9]

Only a general idea can be formed of the arrangement and disposition of the suburb, for exact details are lacking. The original type, however, was universally very simple. There was, of course, a market, always established on the bank of the stream which passed by the locality. This was the junction point of the streets (*plateae*) leading from it towards the gates giving access

[9] In 1042 the church of the burghers at St. Omer was built at the expense of a certain Lambert who was most probably himself a burgher. A. Giry, *Histoire de St. Omer,* Paris, 1877, p. 369.

to the open country. For the merchant suburb was surrounded by defense works, one of its most important features.

These defense works were, of course, absolutely necessary in a society where, despite the efforts of the princes and the Church, violence and rapine continued to be in universal evidence. Before the dissolution of the Carolingian Empire and the Norseman invasions, the monarchy had succeeded fairly well in guaranteeing public security, and as a result the *portus* of that time, or at least the greater number of them, remained unfortified. But by the second half of the ninth century there no longer existed any guarantee for the safety of personal property, other than the protection of ramparts. A capitulary of 845-856 clearly indicates that the rich men and the few merchants who still were left sought refuge in the towns. The new prosperity of trade attracted the attention of highwaymen of all sorts to such an extent that mercantile centers felt a pressing need for adequate protection against them. Just as merchants did not venture on the highways unless armed, so also they made of their collective residences a sort of stronghold. The settlements which they founded at the foot of the towns or burgs bring to mind the close parallel existing in the forts and the blockhouses built by the European immigrants in the seventeenth and eighteenth centuries in the colonies of America and Canada. Like the latter, they were customarily defended merely by a solid palisade of wood pierced with gates and surrounded by a moat. An interesting souvenir of these first urban fortifications survives in the custom, long preserved in heraldry, of symbolizing a city by a sort of circular hedge.

It is certain that this rude enclosure of timber had no other purpose than the parrying of unexpected attacks. It constituted a security against bandits; it would not have been able to withstand a regular siege.[10] In case of war it had to be abandoned and put to the torch in order to prevent the enemy from turning it to his own ends, while refuge was sought in the stronger citadel of a town or burg. It was not until about the beginning of the twelfth century that the growing prosperity of the merchant colonies enabled them to make their security somewhat more certain by building solid ramparts of stone, flanked by towers, and capable of facing a serious attack. Thereafter they became fortresses in themselves. The old feudal or episcopal enclosure which continued to stand in their center thus lost all reason for existence. Little by little their useless walls were

---

[10] At Bruges, at the beginning of the twelfth century, the town was still defended only by wooden palisades.

allowed to fall in ruin. Houses leaned up against them, and they were broken open to make way for new streets. Very often it happened that the towns bought them back from the count or the bishop, for whom they no longer represented anything but idle capital, demolished them and transferred the ground they had covered into building lots.

In the need of security which the merchants felt there lies, therefore, the explanation of the fundamental characteristic of the towns of the Middle Ages. They were strongholds. It is impossible to imagine a town existing at that era without walls. It was an attribute by which towns were distinguished from villages. It was a right, or, to use the expression of that time, it was a *privilege* which none of them lacked. Here again heraldry conforms very exactly to reality, in surmounting the crests of cities by a walled crown.

But the rampart was not only the symbol of the city; it was from it also that came the name which served and which still serves to designate the population. Because of the very fact that it was a fortified place, the town became a burg. The mercantile center, as has been shown above, was designated by the name of "new burg" to distinguish it from the original "old burg." And hence its inhabitants, at the beginning of the eleventh century at the latest, received the name of

"burghers" (*burgenses*). The first known mention
of this word occurs in France in 1007. It appears
again in Flanders, at St. Omer, in 1056; then it
passes into the Empire by the intermediary of
the region of the Moselle, where it crops up at
Huy in 1066. It was therefore the inhabitants of
the "new burg," that is to say of the merchant
burg, who received, or more probably who created it to describe themselves, the appellation of
"burghers." It is curious to see that it was never
applied to those of the "old burg." These latter
were known as *castellani* or *castrenses*. And this
is further, and particularly significant, proof that
the origins of city populations should be sought
not in the older population of the early fortresses
but in the immigrant population which trade
brought to them and which, in the eleventh century, began to absorb them.

The appellation of "burgher" did not immediately come into universal use. Along with it,
that of *cives* (citizen) was still employed, in conformity with the ancient tradition. In England
and Flanders there are also found the words
poortmanni and *poorters*, both of which fell into
disuse about the end of the Middle Ages but con-
firm in the happiest manner the identity, which
has elsewhere been established, between the *portus*
and the "new burg." Strictly speaking, they were

really one and the same thing, and the synonym-
ity which language shows between the *poort-*
mannus and the *burgensis* would be enough to
attest to it even if sufficient proof had not been
already adduced.

It is somewhat difficult to define this original
middle class of the commercial centers. Evidently
it was not composed exclusively of those wide-
travelled merchants spoken of in the preceding
chapter. It must have comprised, besides them,
a more or less important number of men engaged
in the unloading and the transporting of merchandise, in the rigging and the equipping of the
boats, in the manufacture of carts, casks, chests
or, in a word, of all the necessary accessories for
carrying on business. As a result, men from the
whole neighboring territory were drawn to the
nascent city in search of a profession. A definite
and positive attraction by the urban population
for the rural population is clearly manifest by
the beginning of the eleventh century. The greater
the concentration of population, the greater the
effect it had roundabout. It needed, for its daily
existence, not only a quantity but also an increasing variety of skilled workmen. The few artisans
who heretofore had sufficed for the limited needs
of the towns and the burgs evidently could not
satisfy the multiplied exigencies of the newcomers.

Members of the most indispensable professions therefore had to come from outside—bakers, brewers, butchers, smiths, and so on.

But trade itself stimulated industry. In every region where industry was carried on in the country, trade made a successful effort first to lure it to the city and then to concentrate it there.

Flanders supplies one of the most instructive examples in this respect. It has already been shown that ever since the Celtic era the trade of cloth-making was widely carried on in the country. The peasants, thanks to the preservation of processes and of Roman methods, there manufactured cloth capable of supplying the basis of a regular and profitable export trade. The merchants of the towns did not fail to take advantage thereof. By the end of the tenth century they were shipping cloth to England.[11] They soon learned to know the excellent quality of the native wool and sought to introduce it into Flanders, where they could have it worked up under their supervision. Thus they made themselves givers of work and naturally attracted to the cities the weavers of the country.[12] These weavers thereafter lost their

[11] See above, Chap. IV.

[12] Ghent must have already been an important weaving center in the eleventh century, since the "Vita Macarii," *Monumenta Germaniae historica*, Vol. XV, p. 616, speaks of the proprietors of the neighborhood bringing their wool thither.

rural character and became simple employees in the service of the merchants.

The increase of the population naturally favored industrial concentration. Numbers of the poor poured into the towns where cloth-making, the activity of which trade grew proportionately with the development of commerce, guaranteed them their daily bread. Their condition there, however, seems to have been very miserable. The competition which they maintained with each other in the labor market allowed the merchants to pay them a very low wage. Existing information, of which the earliest dates back to the eleventh century, shows them to have been a brutish lower class, uneducated and discontented. The social conflicts which industrial life must have fomented, and which were so terrible in the Flanders of the thirteenth and fourteenth centuries, were already in embryo in the very period of city evolution. The antagonism between capital and labor is thereby revealed to be as old as the middle class.

The old rural industry very quickly disappeared. It could not compete with that of the town, abundantly supplied with the raw material of commerce, operating at lower prices, and enjoying more advanced methods. For the merchants, with an eye to selling, did not fail to improve the quality of the goods they exported. They organized and themselves directed the workshops where the cloths were milled and dyed. In the twelfth century they had come to be without rivals, in the markets of Europe, for the fineness of their weaves and the beauty of their colors. They increased the dimensions also. The old square "cloaks" (*pallia*) which the weavers of the country districts had formerly made, were replaced by pieces of cloth thirty to sixty ells in length, more economical to make and easier to ship.

The cloths of Flanders thus became one of the most sought-after general articles of merchandise. The concentration of this industry in the towns remained, until the end of the Middle Ages, the chief source of their prosperity and helped to make them virtually great manufacturing centers, of which Douai, Ghent and Ypres were distinctive types.

Although cloth-making was the dominant industry in Flanders it was, naturally, far from being restricted to that country alone. Many of the towns of the north and the south of France, of Italy and Rhenish Germany, were also successfully engaged in it. Cloth, more than any other manufactured product, was the basis of the commerce of the Middle Ages. Metallurgy enjoyed far less importance. It was confined almost en-

tirely to brass-working, to which certain cities,
and particularly Dinant in Belgium, owe their
fortune. But whatever might be the nature of industry in other respects, everywhere it obeyed that
law of concentration which was operative at such
an early date in Flanders. Everywhere the city
groups, thanks to commerce, drew rural industry
to them.[13]

In the era of demesnial economy, each agricultural center, big or little, supplied in the largest
measure possible its own wants. The great proprietor maintained in his "court" artisan-serfs,
just as each peasant built his own house or made
with his own hands the furniture or the utensils he
needed. The peddlers, the Jews, the infrequent
merchants who passed through the markets at
great intervals supplied the rest. They lived under
conditions very similar to those which still exist,
or at least existed until very lately, in many regions of Russia. All this was changed when the
towns began to offer to the rural population industrial products of every sort. It resulted in an
exchange of commodities between the middle
classes and the rural population, as has been
pointed out above. The artisans who supplied the

[13] In the eleventh century the "Miracula Sancti Bavonis," *Monumenta Germaniae historica*, Vol. XV, p. 594, mentioned at Ghent
the *"laici qui ex officio agnominabantur coriarii."* There is no
doubt but that these artisans had come there from without.

town people found in the rural classes another assured clientèle. There came about a sharp division of labor between town and country. The latter gave itself over to agriculture exclusively, the former to industry and commerce, and this state of things was to endure as long as the social order of the Middle Ages. It was, incidentally, much more advantageous to the middle classes than to the peasants.

The towns, therefore, energetically bent their efforts to safeguard it. They never failed to oppose every attempt to introduce industry into the country districts. They jealously watched over the monopoly which guaranteed their existence. It was not until the dawn of the modern era that they were willing to give up an exclusivism no longer compatible with economic progress.

The middle classes whose double activity—commercial and industrial—has just been outlined, were faced by innumerable difficulties which they overcame only as time went on. No provision had been made for their reception in the towns and burgs where they settled down. There they were a cause of perturbation at first, and probably they were very often greeted as undesirables. First of all they had to come to terms with the proprietors of the soil. Sometimes it was the bishop, sometimes a monastery, sometimes a count or a seigneur who owned the land and there administered justice. Frequently it even happened that the space occupied by the *portus* or the "new burg" was amenable to the jurisdiction of several tribunals and of several demesnes. It was intended for agriculture, and the immigration of the new-comers changed it all at once into ground for building. A certain time was needed before the owners perceived the profit they could make out of it. At first they particularly resented the incon-venience caused by the appearance of these col-onies given over to a sort of life which went coun-ter to custom or which shocked traditional ideas.

Conflicts immediately arose. They were inevi-table, in view of the fact that the newcomers, who were strangers, were hardly inclined to value the interests, rights and customs which inconveni-enced them. Room had to be made for them as best as could be done, and as their numbers in-creased their encroachments became more and more bold.

In 1099, at Beauvais, the chapter was obliged to bring action against the dyers who had so ob-structed the course of the river that its mills could no longer function. Elsewhere, from time to time, a bishop or a monastery disputed with the burgh-ers the lands they occupied. But whether they willed or not, they had to come to terms. At Arras the abbey of St. Vaast ended by parting with its tillages and parcelling them out. Similar cases occurred at Ghent and Douai. Despite the penury of existing information, it must be assumed that arrangements of this sort were very common. Even at the present day the names of streets recall, in many cities, the agricultural character which was theirs at the beginning. At Ghent, for example, one of the principal arteries is still designated under the name of "Field Street" (*Veldstraat*) and near it is to be found "Husbandry Square" (*place du Kouter*).[14]

To the multiplicity of proprietors corresponded the multiplicity of forms of government to which the lands were subject. Some were subject to land-taxes and statute-labor, others to prestations destined for the maintenance of the knights who formed the permanent garrison of the "old burg"; still others to dues collected by the castellan or by the bishop or by an attorney under the authority of the chief justiciary. All, in short, bore the stamp of an era in which economic organization, like political organization, had been based entirely on possession of the soil. To that were added the

[14] For the status of real estate in the towns, see G. Des Marez, *Étude sur la propriété foncière dans les villes du Moyen-âge et spécialement en Flandre,* Ghent, 1898. The oldest known reference to the enfranchisement of city land dates back to the beginning of the eleventh century.

formalities and the taxes customarily levied at
the time of the transfer of real estate, and which
singularly complicated, if they did not actually
make impossible, purchase and sale.

Under such conditions the land, burdened by
the accumulated vested interests which weighed
heavily upon it, could not play any part in business operations, acquire a market value, or serve
as a basis of credit.

The multiplicity of jurisdictions complicated
still more a situation already so intricate. It was
rare indeed that the land occupied by the burghers
belonged to only a single seigneur. Each of the
proprietors, among whom it was shared, had his
demesnial court which alone was competent in
matters of real estate. Some of these courts administered, in addition, either high justice or low
justice. The confusion of competencies aggra-
vated still further the confusion of jurisdictions.
The result was that the same man was dependent
at the same time on several tribunals, according
to whether it was a question of debts, of crimes,
or simply of the possession of the land. The difficulties which resulted therefrom were the greater
in that these tribunals were not all held in the
town, and it was sometimes necessary to travel a
long distance to plead before them. Furthermore,
they differed among themselves, in their composi-

tion as well as in the law they administered. Side by side with the demesnial courts there existed almost always an older tribunal of aldermen set up, it might be, either in the town or in the burg. The ecclesiastical court of the diocese drew to it not only matters relevant to canonical law, but even all those in which a member of the clergy was interested, without taking count of the number of questions of successions, civil status, marriage, etc.

A glance at the condition of individuals, makes the complexity seem greater yet. As the composition of the city took form, every contrast and every gradation in the status of individuals was to be found. Nothing could be more bizarre, in fact, than this nascent middle class. The merchants, as has been seen above, were *de facto* free men. But this was not the case with a very great number of the immigrants who, lured by the hope of finding work, flocked to the towns. They were almost always natives of the nearby countryside and so could not dissemble their civil status. The seigneur of the demesne from which they had escaped could easily seek them out and identify them; people from their own village ran into them when they came to town. Their parents were known, and it was therefore evident that they had been born into serfdom, since serfdom was the general status of the rural class. It was therefore impossible for them to claim, like the merchants, a freedom which these latter enjoyed only because their true civil status was unknown. Thus the majority of artisans kept, in the town, the status of serfdom in which they had been born. There was, to be sure, an incompatibility between their new social status and their traditional legal status. They had ceased to be peasants but they were not able to efface the original stain with which serfdom had marked the rural class. If they sought to dissemble it they did not fail to be rudely recalled to reality. It sufficed for their seigneur to claim them; they were obliged to follow him and be returned to the demesne whence they had fled.

The merchants themselves indirectly resented the wrongs of serfdom. If they wished to marry, the woman they chose belonged almost always to the serf class. Only the richest among them could aspire to the honor of espousing the daughter of some knight whose debts he had paid. For the others, their union with a serf would have for its consequence the serfdom of their children. Common law ascribed to children, in fact, the legal status of their mother by virtue of the adage *partus ventrem sequitur,* and it is easy to imagine the absurd consequences which arose out of this principle for families. Marriage caused serfdom to reappear in the household. Rancors and conflicts were inevitably born of so contradictory a situation. The ancient law, in seeking to impose itself upon a social order for which it was not adapted, ended in manifest absurdities and injustices which called irresistibly for reform.

On the other hand, while the middle class grew larger and with its numbers acquired power, the nobility little by little retreated and gave way before it. The knights who were settled in the town or in the burg no longer had any reason for living there after the military importance of these old fortresses had disappeared. There was a distinct tendency, at least in the north of Europe, to retire to the country and to leave the towns. Only in Italy and in the south of France did the nobles continue to have their residences in the town.

This fact must be attributed to the preservation, in those countries, of the traditions and, in a certain measure, of the municipal organization of the Roman Empire. The cities of Italy and Provence had been too intimately a part of the territories of which they were the administrative centers not to have preserved, at the time of the economic decline of the eighth and ninth centuries, closer relations with it than anywhere else. The nobility, whose fiefs were scattered all over the country, did not acquire that rural character which typified the nobility of France, Germany or England. They stayed in the towns, where they lived on the revenues from their lands. There they built, in the late Middle Ages, those towers which today give so picturesque an aspect to so many of the old cities of Tuscany. They did not divest themselves of the urban stamp with which ancient society had been so strongly marked. The contrast between the nobility and the middle class, therefore, appears less striking in Italy than in the rest of Europe. At the era of the commercial revival, the nobles of the cities of Lombardy even interested themselves in the business of the merchants and put some of their income into business enterprises. It is in this way, perhaps, that the development of Italian cities differs most profoundly from that of the cities of the north.

In these last it is only in a quite exceptional case that we find here and there, as if gone astray in the midst of middle class society, a family of knights. In the twelfth century the exodus of the nobility to the country was completed almost everywhere. This is a development, however, which is still very little understood, and it is to be hoped that further researches will throw greater light upon it. Meanwhile it may be assumed that the economic crisis, to which the nobility were prey following the diminution of their revenues in the thirteenth century, was not without its influence in their disappearance from the towns. They must have found it advantageous to sell to the burghers the lands they owned, the altering of which into ground for building had enormously augmented their value.

The status of the clergy was not sensibly modified by the influx of the middle class to the towns and burgs. Out of it arose a few inconveniences for them, but also a few advantages. The bishops had to battle to maintain intact, in the presence of the newcomers, their rights of justice and their rights of demesne; the monasteries and the chapters saw themselves forced to permit houses to be built on their fields or on their tillages. The patriarchal and demesnial form of government to which the Church had been accustomed suddenly found itself at grips with unexpected claims and needs, out of which was to result, at the start, a period of uneasiness and insecurity.

On the other hand, however, compensations were not lacking. The rental or tribute levied on the lots of land given over to the burghers formed an increasingly fruitful source of revenue. The increase in population brought with it a corresponding increase in the perquisites supplied by baptisms, marriages and deaths; the yield from offerings went on increasing unceasingly; merchants and artisans formed pious confraternities affiliated to a church or to a monastery in return for annual dues. The creation of new parishes, proportionately as the number of inhabitants mounted, multiplied the numbers and the resources of the secular clergy. After the beginning of the eleventh century abbeys, on the contrary, were founded in towns only in very exceptional cases. They were not able to accustom themselves to that life, too blustering and busy, and in addition it was no longer possible to find the room necessary for a great religious house with the accessory services it required. The Cistercian Order, which spread so widely through Europe in the course of the twelfth century, organized only in the country.

It was only in the following century that the monks were to come back to the towns again. The mendicant friars, Franciscans and Dominicans, who were to come and settle there, were not merely a normal development arising from the new orientation which religious fervor took. The principle of poverty which they professed made them break with the demesnial organization, heretofore the support of monastic life. By them monasticism was found to be wonderfully well adapted to a city atmosphere. They asked no more of the burghers than their alms. In place of isolating themselves in the center of vast, silent enclosures, they built their convents along the streets. They took part in all the agitations, all the miseries as well, and understood all the aspirations of the artisans, whose spiritual directors they well deserved to become.

Chapter VII

Municipal Institutions

CITIES, in their formative period, found themselves in a singularly complicated situation. They were faced with problems of all sorts. In them there existed side by side two populations which did not mix, and which presented all the contrasts of two distinct worlds. The old demesnial organization with all the traditions, all the opinions, all the ideas which may not have been born of it but which received from it their particular stamp, came to grips with wants and aspirations which had taken it by surprise, which went counter to its interests, to which it was not adapted and which, from the very first, it opposed. If it gave ground, that was in spite of itself and because the new conditions which had to be faced were due to causes too profound and irresistible for their effect not to be felt.

The consequences of facts which are so little affected by human wishes as the increase of population and the expansion of trade could not be avoided. Probably those in positions of authority in the social order were not able to appreciate the import of the changes that were taking place about them. The old order of things sought, at first, to maintain its position. Only later, and usually too late, did it try to adapt itself. As always happens, the change did not come about all at once. And it would be improper to attribute, as has frequently been done, to "feudal tyranny" or to "sacerdotal arrogance" an opposition which is to be explained by more natural incentives. There happened in the Middle Ages what has happened so often since then. Those who were the beneficiaries of the established order were bent upon defending it, not so much, perhaps, because it guaranteed their interests, as because it seemed to them indispensable to the preservation of society.

It should be borne in mind, moreover, that this social order the middle classes accepted. Their demands and what might be called their political program did not aim in any way at its abolition; they took for granted the privileges and the authority of the princes, the clergy, and the nobility. They merely wished to obtain, because it was necessary to their existence, not an overthrow of the existing order but simple concessions. And these concessions were limited to their own needs. They were completely uninterested in those of the rural population from which they had sprung. In short, they only asked of society to make for them a place compatible with the sort of life they were leading. They were not revolutionary, and if they happened to turn to violence it was not through hate against the government but quite simply to force compliance.

A brief review of the principal points in their program will be enough to show that they did not go beyond an indispensable minimum. What they wanted, first of all, was personal liberty, which would assure to the merchant or the artisan the possibility of going and coming, of living where he wished and of putting his own person as well as that of his children under the protection of the seigniorial power. Next came the creation of a special tribunal by means of which the burgher would at one stroke escape the multiplicity of jurisdictions to which he was amenable and the inconveniences which the formalistic procedure of ancient law imposed upon his social and economic activity. Then came the instituting in the city of a "peace"—that is to say, of a penal code—which would guarantee security. And then came the abolition of those prestations most incompatible with the carrying on of trade and industry, and with the possession and acquisition of land. What they wanted, in fine, was a more or less extensive degree of political autonomy and local self-government.

All of this was very far from forming a coherent whole and being based on theoretical principles. Nothing was further from the mind of the original middle classes than any conception of the rights of man and citizen. Personal liberty itself was not claimed as a natural right. It was sought only for the advantages it conferred. This is so true that at Arras, for example, the merchants tried to have themselves classed as serfs of the Monastery of St. Vast in order to enjoy the exemption from the market-tolls which had been accorded to the latter.

It was not until the beginning of the eleventh century that the first direct action was taken by the middle classes against the order of things they suffered from. Their efforts thereafter never halted. Despite vicissitudes and reverses, the movement of reform advanced unhesitatingly towards its goal, broke by main force, if necessary, the opposition that stood in the way and ended, in the course of the twelfth century, by giving the towns those essentially municipal institutions which were to be the basis of their constitutions.

Everywhere it was the merchants who took the initiative and directed events. Nothing was more natural than that. They were the most active, the

richest, the most influential element in the city
population and they endured with so much the
more impatience a situation which clashed with
their interests and sapped their confidence in
themselves. The rôle they then played, despite the
enormous difference in time and conditions, may
fittingly be compared with that which the capitalistic middle class assumed after the end of the
eighteenth century in the political revolution
which put an end to the old order of things. In the
one case as in the other, the social group which
was the most directly interested in the change assumed the leadership of the opposition, and was
followed by the masses. Democracy in the Middle
Ages, as in modern times, got its start under the
guidance of a select few who foisted their program
upon the confused aspirations of the people.

The episcopal cities were the first to be the scene
of combat. It would be a decided mistake to attribute this fact to the personality of the bishops.
A great number of them distinguished themselves,
on the contrary, by their manifest solicitude for
the public weal. Excellent administrators, whose
memory has remained with the people throughout
the centuries, were by no means rare among them.
At Liège, for example, Notger (972-1018) attacked the castles of the robber barons who in-
fested the neighborhood, and turned from its

course a branch of the Meuse to make the city more healthy and to strengthen its fortifications.

Similar examples could easily be cited in the case of Cambrai, Utrecht, Cologne, Worms, Mainz and a number of cities of Germany where the emperors strove, up to the time of the investiture struggle, to name prelates notable equally for their intelligence and their energy.

But the more the bishops were conscious of their duties, the more also they had to defend their government against the demands of their subjects and endeavor to keep them under an authoritative, patriarchal regimen. The confusion of spiritual power and temporal power in their hands, moreover, caused every concession to seem to them to be a peril to the Church. It must also not be forgotten that their functions obliged them to reside permanently in their cities and that they feared, with good reason, the difficulties which would be caused them by the autonomy of the burghers in whose midst they lived. Finally, it has already been seen that the Church had little sympathy with trade. This unsympathetic attitude must naturally have made the Church deaf to the wishes of the merchants and of the people who were grouped behind them, have prevented an understanding of their wants, and given a false impression of their real power. Out of this came misunderstandings, clashes, and soon an open hostility which, after the beginning of the eleventh century, was to end in the inevitable.[1]

The movement began in Northern Italy. There, commercial life was older and there the political consequences of it were likewise earlier. Unfortunately very few details are known concerning these events. It is certain that the troubles to which the Church was then prey could hardly have delayed their precipitation. The inhabitants of the towns sided passionately with the monks and the priests who were waging a campaign against the evil customs of the clergy, attacking simony and the marriage of priests, and condemning the intervention of lay authority in the administration of the Church, to the profit of the papacy. The bishops, named by the emperor and compromised by that fact in itself, thus found themselves face to face with an opposition in which mysticism, the claims of the merchants and the discontent caused by the misery of the industrial workers were allied and mutually strengthened. It is certain that the nobles took part in the agitation, for it gave them the opportunity to shake off episcopal suzerainty, and made common cause with the burghers and the patarenes—the

[1] We find in the English clergy the same hostility towards the middle class, as in the German and French clergy.

name by which the conservatives contemptuously designated their adversaries.

In 1057 Milan, even then the queen of the cities of Lombardy, was in open revolt against the archbishop. The vicissitudes of the investiture struggle naturally spread the disturbances and gave them a turning more and more favorable to the insurgents, proportionately as the cause of the pope got the better of that of the emperor. There were established, either by the consent of the bishops or by force, magistrates with the title of "consuls" and charged with the administration of the towns. The first of these consuls to be mentioned, but probably not the first to exist, appear at Lucca in 1080. There is a record as early as 1068 of a "communal court" in that city, a characteristic feature of city autonomy which surely must have existed at the same date in plenty of other places. The consuls of Milan are not cited before 1107, but they were surely much earlier in origin than that. From the time they are first mentioned, they show the distinctive physiognomy of communal magistrates. They were recruited among divers social classes—among the *capitanei*, the *valvassores*, and the *cives*—and represented the *communio civitatis*.

The most typical feature of this magistracy was its yearly character, wherein it was in distinct contrast to the offices for life which alone the feudal régime knew. This yearly feature of the offices was the consequence of their elective nature. In laying hold of power, the city population entrusted it to delegates named by itself. Thus was affirmed the principle of control at the same time as that of election. Municipal democracy, from its first attempts at organization, created the instruments necessary to its proper functioning and unhesitatingly set foot on the path which has been followed ever since.

From Italy, the "consulate" soon spread to the cities of Provence, evident proof of its perfect adaptation to the needs which were felt by the middle class. Marseilles had consuls at the start of the twelfth century, or at the latest by 1128; we find them next at Arles and at Nimes, until little by little they spread in the south of France as commerce made headway from place to place and, with it, the political transformation which it brought in tow.

Nearly at the same time as in Italy, municipal institutions arose in the region of Flanders and the north of France. There is nothing surprising in this, since that country, like Lombardy, had been the scene of vigorous commercial activity. Fortunately the sources of information here are more abundant and more precise. They make it possible to follow fairly accurately the march of events.

It is not the episcopal cities alone which here hold the stage. Side by side with them are to be observed other centers of activity, though it is within their walls that were formed those communes whose nature it is most important to consider. The oldest, and fortunately also the best known, is that of Cambrai.

During the eleventh century the prosperity of this city was well advanced. At the foot of the original town clustered a commercial suburb, which had been surrounded in 1070 by a wall. The population of this suburb endured with scant patience the authority of the bishop and his castellan. It prepared in secret for revolt when, in 1077, Bishop Gerard II had to absent himself to go receive in Germany the investiture at the hands of the emperor. He was hardly en route before, under the direction of the richest merchants of the town, the people arose, took possession of the gates and proclaimed a commune. The poor, the artisans, and the weavers, in particular, launched themselves still more passionately into the fray when a reformer-priest called Ramihrdus denounced to them the bishop as a simoniac and inspired in the depths of their hearts the mysticism which, at that same era, was arousing the

Lombard patarenes. As in Italy, religious fervor lent its strength to the political demands and the commune was sworn in the midst of general enthusiasm.

This commune of Cambrai was the oldest of all that are known north of the Alps. It seems to have been both a fighting organization and an instrument of public safety. It was necessary, in fact, to await the return of the bishop and to prepare to cope with him. The need of unanimous action was imperative. An oath was exacted from all, establishing among them the necessary solidarity, and it was this association, sworn to by the burghers on the eve of battle, which was the essential characteristic of that first commune.

Its success, however, was only ephemeral. The bishop, upon receiving the news, hastened back and succeeded in restoring his authority for the time being. But the experiment of the Cambresians was not long in being imitated. The following years were marked by the establishment of communes in the majority of the towns of Northern France; at St. Quentin about 1080, at Beauvais about 1099, at Noyon in 1108-1109, at Laon in 1115. During the initial period the middle class and the bishops lived in a state of permanent hostility and, as it were, on the point of open war. Force alone was able to prevail between such adversaries, equally convinced of their due rights. Ives of Chartres exhorted the bishops not to give ground and to consider as void the promises which, under the threat of violence, they had happened to make to the burghers. Guibert of Nogent, on his part, spoke with mingled contempt and fear of those "pestilential communes" which the serfs had set up against their lords, to escape authority and to do away with the most legitimate rights.

In spite of all, however, the communes prevailed. Not only did they have the strength that numbers give, but the monarchy which in France, starting with the reign of Louis VI, was beginning to regain lost ground, interested itself in their cause. Just as the popes, in their conflict with the German emperors, had relied upon the patarenes of Lombardy, so the Capetian monarchs of the twelfth century favored the efforts of the middle classes.

There can probably be no question of ascribing to them a political principle. At first glance their conduct seems full of contradictions. Yet it is none the less true that they evinced a general tendency to take the part of the towns. The clear interest of the monarchy was to support the adversaries of high feudalism. Naturally, help was given whenever it was possible to do so without becoming obligated to these middle classes who in arising against their lords fought, to all intents and purposes, in the interests of royal prerogatives. To accept the king as arbitrator of their quarrel was, for the parties in conflict, to recognize his sovereignty. The entry of the burghers upon the political scene had as a consequence the weakening of the contractual principle of the Feudal State to the advantage of the principle of the authority of the Monarchial State. It was impossible that royalty should not take count of this and seize every chance to show its good-will to the communes which, without intending to do so, labored so usefully in its behalf.

In specially designating by the name of "communes" those episcopal cities of the north of France where municipal institutions were the result of insurrection, it is well to exaggerate neither their importance nor their originality. There is no reason for claiming that there was any essential difference between commune-cities and other cities. They were distinguished from one another only by incidental characteristics. At bottom their nature was the same, and in reality all were equally communes. In all of them, in fact, the burghers formed a corps, a *universitas*, a *communitas,* a *communio*, all the members of which, conjointly answerable to one another, constituted the inseparable parts. Whatever might be the ori-

gin of its enfranchisement, the city of the Middle
Ages did not consist in a simple collection of individuals; it was itself an individual, but a collective individual, a legal person. All that can
be claimed in favor of the communes *stricto sensu*
is a particular distinctiveness of institutions, a
clearly established separation of the rights of the
bishop and those of the burghers, and a manifest
preoccupation to safeguard the rights of the latter
by a powerful corporate organization. But all of
that derived from the circumstances which presided over the birth of the communes. Although
they preserved the traces of their insurrectionary
composition, it does not necessarily follow that
they should be assigned, for that reason, a special
place in the ensemble of cities. It can even be
observed that certain ones among them enjoyed
prerogatives less extensive, a jurisdiction and an
autonomy less complete, than those of localities
in which the commune was only the mark of the
advent of a peaceful evolution. It is a manifest
error to reserve for them, as is sometimes, done,
the name of "collective seigniories." We shall see
later that all fully developed cities were such seigniories.

Violence, therefore, was far from being an essential factor in the creation of municipal institutions. In the majority of towns subject to the

power of a lay prince, their growth was accomplished, in general, without need of recourse to
force. And it is not necessary to attribute this situation to the particular good-will which the lay
princes had shown towards political liberty. On
the other hand all the incentives which inspired
the bishop to oppose the burghers carried no
weight with the princes. They professed no hostility in regard to trade; on the contrary, they
were experiencing its good effects. It increased
traffic in their territories, and by that very fact
augmented the revenues from their tolls and the
activity of their mints which were forced to meet
an increasing demand for currency. Having no
spot as capital and incessantly travelling about
their demesnes, they lived in their towns only at
rare intervals and therefore had no reason for
quarreling with the burghers over the administration of them. It is quite characteristic that Paris,
the only city which before the end of the twelfth
century could be considered a real capital, did not
succeed in obtaining an autonomous municipal
constitution. But the interest which impelled the
King of France to keep control of his customary
residence was completely lacking with the dukes
and counts, as peripatetic as the king was seden-
tary. Lastly, they did not view altogether with
displeasure the act of the burghers in seizing the

power from the castellans who had become an
hereditary class and whose strength was a cause
of uneasiness to them. They had, in short, the
same incentives as the King of France for looking
with favor upon these tendencies, since they weakened the status of their vassals. It is not on record,
however, that they systematically lent them their
aid. They confined themselves, in general, to letting them alone and their attitude was almost always one of benevolent neutrality.

No region offers a better chance for studying
municipal origins in a purely lay environment
than does Flanders. In this great country, which
stretched from the shores of the North Sea and the
Zealand Islands to the frontiers of Normandy,
the episcopal cities never rivalled in importance
and wealth the commercial and industrial cities.
Térouanne, the diocese of which comprised the
watershed of the Yser, was and always remained
a half-rural hamlet. Arras and Tournai, which
extended their spiritual jurisdiction over the rest
of the territory, developed to an appreciable extent
only in the course of the twelfth century. On the
contrary, Ghent, Bruges, Ypres, St. Omer, Lille
and Douai, where were gathered together in the
course of the tenth century active merchant colonies, give an unusually clear picture of the birth
of municipal institutions. They lend themselves

to this so much the better in that, all being organized in the same way and showing the same characteristics, the information of which each gives us its share can be safely combined into one general picture.

All these cities show, first, the distinctive feature of having been organized around a central burg which was, so to speak, their nucleus. At the foot of this burg was grouped a *portus*, or "new burg," populated by merchants to whose numbers were soon added artisans, either free or serf, and where, after the eleventh century, the textile industry came to be concentrated. Over the burg as over the *portus* extended the authority of the castellan. More or less important parcels of land occupied by the immigrant population belonged to the abbeys, others to the Count of Flanders. A tribunal of aldermen had its seat in the burg under the presidency of the castellan. This tribunal had in other respects no competency relative to the city. Its jurisdiction extended over all the castellany of which the burg was the center, and the members who composed it resided in that same castellany and came to the burg only on the days of hearings. For ecclesiastical jurisdiction, to which were amenable a number of matters, it was necessary to go to the episcopal court of the diocese.

A variety of obligations weighed upon the land and the inhabitants, whether of the burg or of the *portus*: ground rents, prestations in money or in kind destined for the upkeep of the knights charged with the defense of the burg, and tolls levied on all merchandise brought by land or water.

All this was of long standing, created at the height of the demesnial and feudal régime, and was in no way adapted to the new needs of the merchant population. Not being made for it, the organization which had its seat in the burg not only rendered no service but on the contrary interfered with activities. The survivals of the past bore down with all their weight upon the needs of the present. Obviously, for reasons which have been given above and to which it is unnecessary to return, the middle class felt far from content and exacted the reforms necessary to their free expansion.

In these reforms it devolved upon them to take the initiative, for they could not rely on either the castellans, the monasteries, or the barons whose lands they occupied, to bring them about. But it was also necessary, in the midst of a population so heterogeneous as that of the *portus*, for a group of men to take control of the mass and to have enough power and prestige to give it direction. The merchants, in the first half of the eleventh century, resolutely assumed this rôle. Not only did they constitute the wealthiest element in each town, the most active and the most desirous of change, but they had in addition the strength that union gives. The needs of commerce early impelled them, as has been seen above, to organize in confraternities called gilds or hanses—autonomous corporations independent of all authority and in which their will alone made the law. Freely elected chiefs, "deans" or "counts of the hanse" (*Dekanen, Hansgrafen*), supervised the maintenance of a voluntarily accepted discipline. At regular intervals the colleagues assembled to drink and deliberate over their interests; a treasury, supported by their contributions, provided for the needs of the society; a community house (*Gildhalle*) served as the place of their meetings. Such was the Gild of St. Omer, about 1050, and it may be assumed from this instance that very probably similar associations existed at the same period in all the merchant colonies of Flanders.

The prosperity of trade was so intimately bound up with the organization of the towns in which it had located that the members of the gild were almost automatically charged with making provision for the needs that were most pressing. The castellans had no reason to restrain them from meeting, through their own resources, those emergencies that were clearly apparent. They permitted them to "extemporize," as it were, in official communal administration. At St. Omer an arrangement made between the gild and the castellan, Wulfric Rabel (1072-1083), permitted the former to attend to the cases of the burghers. Thus, without having any legal warrant therefor, the merchant association devoted itself of its own accord to the organization and the management of the nascent city. It made up for the impotence of public power. At St. Omer the gild devoted a part of its revenues to the construction of defense works and to the maintenance of the streets. There is no doubt but that other Flemish towns, its neighbors, did the same. The name of "counts of the hanse" which the treasurers of the city of Lille kept all through the Middle Ages is sufficient proof, in the absence of other records, that there also the chiefs of the voluntary corporation of merchants drew upon the treasury of the gild for the benefit of their fellow citizens. At Audenarde the name of *Hansgraf* was borne up to the fourteenth century by a magistrate of the commune. At Tournai, as late as the thirteenth century, city finances were placed under the control of the *Charité St. Christophe,* that is to say of the merchant gild. At Bruges the contributions of the "brothers of the hanse" supported the municipal treasury up until its disappearance at the time of the democratic revolution of the fourteenth century.

The result of all this, manifestly, was that the gilds were, in the region of Flanders, the initiators of city autonomy. Of their own accord they charged themselves with a task which no one else had been able to carry out. Officially they had no right to act as they did; their intervention is to be explained solely by the cohesion which existed among their members, by the influence their group enjoyed, by the resources they disbursed, and finally by the understanding they had of the collective needs of the middle-class population. It can be stated, without exaggeration, that in the course of the eleventh century the chiefs of the gild performed, *de facto,* the functions of communal magistrates in every town.

They were doubtless the ones, also, who led the counts of Flanders to take an interest in the development and the prosperity of the towns. In 1043 Baldwin IV obtained from the monks of St. Omer the concession on the basis of which the burghers built their church. At the beginning of the reign of Robert the Friesian (1071-1093), exemptions from tolls, grants of land, privileges limiting the episcopal jurisdiction or the requirements of military service were granted in considerable number to the cities then in process of formation. Robert of Jerusalem favored the city of Aire with "liberties" and exempted, in 1111, the burghers of Ypres from the judiciary duel.

The result of all this was that little by little the middle class stood out as a distinct and privileged group in the midst of the population of the country. From a simple social group given over to the carrying on of commerce and industry, it was transformed into a legal group, recognized as such by the princely power. And out of that legal status itself was to come, necessarily, the granting of an independent legal organization. The new law needed as its organ a new tribunal. The old aldermanic district courts, sitting in the burgs and administering justice in accordance with a custom that had become archaic and incapable of accommodating its rigid formalism to the needs of a community for which it had not been created, had to give way to courts whose members, recruited from among the burghers, were able to render them a justice adequate to their desires and conforming to their aspirations—a justice, in fine, which was *their* justice. It is impossible to say exactly when this important development took place. The oldest reference in Flanders to an aldermanic court—

that is to say of such a court peculiar to one city—
dates back to the year 1111 and has to do with
Arras. But there is nothing to prevent the assump-
tion that aldermanic courts of this kind must have
already existed at the same period in the more important localities such as Ghent, Bruges or Ypres.
Whatever may have been the case elsewhere, the
beginning of the twelfth century saw this decided
innovation come to pass in all the cities of Flanders. The disturbances which followed the assas-
sination of Count Charles the Good, in 1127, permitted the burghers to realize in full their political
program. The pretenders to the county, William
of Normandy, and later Thierry of Alsace, in
order to rally them to their cause conceded to them
the demands they addressed.

The charter granted to St. Omer in 1127 may be
considered as the point of departure of the political program of the burghers of Flanders. It recognized the city as a distinct legal territory, provided
with a special law common to all inhabitants, with
special aldermanic courts and a full communal
autonomy. Other charters in the course of the
twelfth century ratified similar grants to all the
principal cities of the county. Their status was
thereafter secured and sanctioned by written
warrants.

On the other hand care must be taken not to attribute to the city charters an exaggerated importance. Neither in Flanders nor in any other region of Europe did they embrace the whole of the city law. They limited themselves to fixing the principal outlines, to formulating some of the essential principles, to settling a few particularly important conflicts. Most of the time they were the product of special circumstances and they took count only of matters which were under debate at the time they were drawn up. They cannot be considered as the result of systematic planning and legislative deliberation similar to that out of which are born, for example, modern constitutions. If the middle classes have kept watch over them throughout the centuries, with an extraordinary solicitude, preserving them under triple lock in chests of iron and surrounding them with a quasi-superstitious respect, it is because they considered them as the palladium of their liberty. It is because they permitted them, in case of violation, to justify their rebellion, but it is not because they included the whole of their rights. They were not, so to speak, more than the framework of the latter. Round about their stipulations existed and continued unceasingly to develop a thick overgrowth of rights, usages, and unwritten but none the less indispensable privileges. This is so true that a number of charters themselves foresaw and recognized in advance the further development of city law. The chronicler Galbert informs us that the Count of Flanders accorded to the burghers of St. Omer in 1127: *"ut die in diem consuetudinarias leges suas corrigerent"*—that is to say, the power of correcting from day to day their municipal laws. There was, therefore, more in the law of the city than what was contained in the terms of the charters. They specified merely fragments of it. They were full of gaps; they were concerned with neither order nor system. We need not expect to find in them the fundamental principles out of which came later evolutions, as for example, Roman law evolved from the law of the Twelve Tables.

It is possible, however, in examining their principles and supplementing one by another, to characterize in its general traits the city law of the Middle Ages as it developed in the course of the twelfth century in the different regions of Western Europe. There is no need to take account, since we are seeking only to trace the general outline, either of the difference in States or even in nations. City law was a phenomenon of the same nature as, for example, that of feudalism. It was the consequence of a social and economic situation common to all peoples. Taking it by regions, there are of course numerous differences in detail. But at bottom it was everywhere the same and it is solely concerning this permanent basis that we shall deal in the following paragraphs.

The first thing which should be considered is the status of the individual as it was when city law was definitely evolved. That status was one of freedom. It is a necessary and universal attribute of the middle class. Each city established a "franchise" in this respect. Every vestige of rural serfdom disappeared within its walls. Whatever might be the differences and even the contrasts which wealth set up between men, all were equal as far as civil status was concerned. "The air of the city makes free," says the German proverb (*Die Stadtluft macht frei*), and this truth held good in every clime. Freedom, of old, used to be the monopoly of a privileged class. By means of the cities it again took its place in society as a natural attribute of the citizen. Hereafter it was enough to reside on city soil to acquire it. Every serf who had lived for a year and a day within the city limits had it by definite right: the statute of limitations abolished all rights which his lord exercised over his person and chattels. Birth meant little. Whatever might be the mark with which it had stigmatized the infant in his cradle, it vanished in the atmosphere of the city. This freedom, which at the beginning only merchants had enjoyed *de facto*, was now the common right of all the burghers *de jure.*

If a few serfs could still exist, here and there among them, they were not members of the city population. They were hereditary servitors of the abbeys or of the seigniories which retained in the cities bits of land not subject to city law and where the old state of things was prolonged. Burgher and freeman had become synonymous terms. Freedom, in the Middle Ages, was an attribute as inseparable from the rank of citizen of a city as it is in our day of that of the citizen of a State.

With freedom of person there went on equal footing, in the city, the freedom of the land. In fact, in a merchant community, land could not remain idle and be kept out of commerce by unwieldy and diverse laws that prevented its free conveyance and restrained it from serving as a means of credit and acquiring capital value. This was the more inevitable in that land, within the city, changed its nature—it became ground for building. It was rapidly covered with houses, crowded one against the other, and increased in value in proportion as they multiplied. Thus it automatically came about that the owner of a house acquired in the course of time the ownership, or at least the possession, of the soil upon which it was built. Everywhere the old demesnial land was

transformed into "censal estate," or "censal allo-
dium." City hold thus became free hold. He who
occupied it was not bound by more than the land
taxes due to the owner of the land, when he did not
happen to be himself the owner. He could freely
transfer it, convey it, mortgage it and make it serve
as security for capital he might borrow. In selling
a mortgage on his house, the burgher procured the
liquid capital he needed; in buying a mortgage on
the house of another, he assured himself of an income proportionate to the sum expended. He
placed, as we would say today, his money out at
interest. Compared to the old feudal or demesnial
tenures, tenure in city law—tenure in *Weichbild*
or *Burgrecht* as they called it in Germany, or
bourgage in France—thus showed a well marked
individuality.

Subject to new economic conditions, city land
ended by acquiring a new law, suited to its nature.
The old land-courts probably did not abruptly disappear. The enfranchisement of the soil did not
have as consequence the spoliation of the old proprietors. Very often they kept, when it was not
bought back from them, portions of the land of
which they had been lords. But the seigniory which
they still exercised over them no longer carried
with it the personal dependence of the tenants.

City law not only did away with personal servitude and restrictions on land, but also caused the disappearance of the seigniorial rights and fiscal claims which interfered with the activity of commerce and industry. The market-tolls (*teloneum*) which were such a handicap to the free circulation of goods were particularly odious to the burghers, and they early made the effort to get rid of them. The chronicler Galbert shows that this was, in Flanders in 1127, one of their chief preoccupations. It was because the pretender, William of Normandy, did not keep his promise in this particular that they rose against him and called Thierry of Alsace. In the course of the twelfth century, everywhere, voluntarily or under compulsion, the market-tolls were modified. Here, they were bought off by means of an annual fee; there, the manner of levying them was changed. In almost every case they were placed under the supervision, and subject to the jurisdiction, of the city authorities. It was the city's magistrates who henceforth took charge of supervising trade and who took the place of the castellans and the old demesnial functionaries in the standardization of weights and measures and in the judical administration of markets and industry generally.

If the market-tolls were modified in passing under the authority of the city, it was otherwise with

the other seigniorial rights which, incompatible
with the free functioning of the life of the city,
were inevitably condemned to disappear altogether. Mention might be made of the surviving
characteristics of the agricultural era which had
been left impressed on the physiognomy of the
city: common ovens and mills, at which the
seigneur compelled the inhabitants to grind their
wheat and bake their bread; monopolies of every
sort, by virtue of which he enjoyed the privilege of
selling at certain periods, without competition, the
wine from his vineyards or the meat from his cattle; the right of shelter, which imposed upon the
burghers the obligation of furnishing him lodging
and subsistence during his stays in the city; the
right of requisition, by which he appropriated to
his service the boats or the horses of the inhabitants; the right of summons to arms, imposing the
obligation of following him to war; customs of
every sort and every origin which had become
oppressive and vexatious because they had long
since become useless, such as that which forbade
the building of bridges over the water courses or
that which compelled the inhabitants to assist in
the maintenance of the knights composing the
garrison of the "old burg." Of all this there remained, at the end of the twelfth century, hardly
more than the memory. The lords, after having

tried resistance, finished by giving way. They realized, in the course of time, that their manifest interest commanded them not to hinder the development of the cities, in order to preserve a few meagre revenues, but to favor it by doing away with the obstacles that stood in its path. They began by taking count of the incompatibility of these old prestations with the new state of things, and they ended by themselves qualifying them as "plunderings and extortions."

Like the status of individuals, the governing of the land, and the fiscal system, the fundamental character of the law itself underwent a transformation in the cities. The complicated and formalistic procedure, the compurgations, the ordeals, the judiciary duel—all these crude methods of proof which too often let chance or sheer luck decide the issue of a trial, were not long, in their turn, in adapting themselves to the new conditions of a city environment. The old rigid forms of contract, which custom had established, disappeared as rapidly as economic life became more complicated and active. The judiciary duel evidently could not be long retained in the midst of a population of merchants and artisans. Proof through witnesses was likewise early substituted in place of proof through compurgators, before the city magistracy bench. The *Wergild,* the old blood-price, gave way to a system of fines and corporal punishments. Finally, legal delays, originally so long, were considerably reduced.

It was not only procedure that was modified. The very content of the law evolved in parallel fashion. In questions of marriage, succession, liens, debts, mortgages, and particularly in questions of business law, a whole new body of legislation was coming into being in the cities, and the jurisprudence of their tribunals created a civil practice, increasingly amplified and exact.

City law was characterized no less from the criminal point of view than from the civil. In such aggregations as the cities were, of men from every station in life, in this environment where abounded wanderers, vagabonds and adventurers, a rigorous discipline was necessary to the maintenance of security. It was equally necessary for intimidating the thieves and bandits who, in every civilization, are drawn towards commercial centers. This is so true that as early as the Carolingian era the towns, within the walls of which the wealthy class sought shelter, seemed to enjoy a special "peace." This is that same word "peace" which was used in the twelfth century to designate the criminal law of the city.

This city peace was a law of exception, more severe, more harsh, than that of the country districts.

It was prodigal of corporal punishments: hanging, decapitation, castration, amputation of limbs. It applied in all its rigor the *lex talionis*: an eye for an eye, a tooth for a tooth. Its evident purpose was to repress derelictions, through terror. All who entered the gates of the city, whether nobles, freemen or burghers, were equally subject to it. Under it the city was, so to speak, in a permanent state of siege. But in it the city found a potent instrument of unification, because it was superimposed upon the jurisdictions and seigniories which shared the soil; it forced its pitiless regulation on all. More than community of interests and residence, it contributed to make uniform the status of all the inhabitants located within the city walls and to create the middle class. The burghers were essentially a group of *homines pacis*—men of the peace. The peace of the city (*pax villae*) was at the same time the law of the city (*lex villae*). The emblems which symbolized the jurisdiction and the autonomy of the city were above all emblems of peace: such as were, for example, the cross or the symbolic set of stone steps in the market-place, the belfries (*Bergfried*), the towers of which arose from the heart of the cities of the Netherlands and Northern France, and the statues of Roland, which were so numerous in Northern Germany.

By virtue of the peace with which it was endowed, the city formed a distinct legal district. The legal principle of territoriality carried with it that of personality. Equally subject to the same penal law, the burghers inevitably shared, sooner or later, in the same civil law. The practice of the city was extended up to the limits of the peace and the city formed, within the circumference of its ramparts, a community of law.

The peace, on the other hand, contributed largely in making the city a commune. It had, in effect, the oath as its sanction. It supposed a *conjuratio* of all the city population. And the oath taken by the burgher was not confined to a simple promise of obedience to municipal authority. It involved strict obligations and imposed a strict duty to maintain and respect the peace. Every *juratus*— that is to say, every burgher sworn—was obliged to lend a helping hand to any burgher calling for help. Thus the peace created, among all its members, a permanent solidarity. Hence the term "brothers" by which they were sometimes designated, or the word *amicitia* used at Lille, for example, as synonym for *pax*. And since the peace covered the whole city population, the latter, therefore, was a commune. The very names which the municipal magistrates bore in a number of places, —"warders of the peace" at Verdun, "reward of friendship" at Lille, "jurors of the peace" at Valenciennes, Cambrai and many other cities— make it easy to see the close relationship between the peace and the commune.

Other causes naturally contributed to the birth of city communes. The most potent among them was the need, early felt by the burghers, of a tax system. Funds were necessary for public works of the most pressing nature, and, above all, for the construction of the city wall. Everywhere the need of building this protecting rampart was the point of departure for city finances. In the cities of the region of Liège the communal tax bore the characteristic name of *firmitas* ("firmness"). At Angers the oldest municipal accounts were those of the *"clouaison, fortification et emparement"* of the city. Elsewhere part of the fines were appropriated *ad opus castri*—for the improvement of the fortifications.

Taxes, naturally, provided the means of securing the needed resources. To subject the taxpayers thereto, recourse had to be had to compulsion. Everyone was obliged to participate, according to his means, in the expenses incurred in the interests of all. Whoever refused to support the charges which they involved was barred from the city. The latter was therefore a commune, an obligatory association, a moral personality. According to the phrase of Beaumanoir, it formed a *"compaignie, laquelle ne pot partir ne desseurer, ançois convient qu'elle tiègne, voillent les parties ou non qui en la compaignie sont."* That is to say, a society which could not be dissolved, but which must needs exist independently of the wishes of its members.

Thus the city of the Middle Ages was simultaneously a legal district and a commune.

There remain to be examined the agencies by which were met the demands its nature imposed.

First of all, inasmuch as it was an independent legal district, it by all means had to have its own jurisdiction. City law being bounded by the city walls, in contrast to the regional law, the law of without, a special tribunal had to be charged with applying it and the burghers had to have, in consequence, the assurance of their privileged status. This is a clause which is lacking in hardly any municipal charter: that the burghers could be tried only by their own magistrates. The latter, as a necessary consequence, were recruited from their midst. It was essential that they be members of the commune and naturally the latter, to a greater or less degree, took part in their nomination. Here, it had the right of designating them to the seigneur; there, the more liberal system of election was applied; still elsewhere, recourse was had to complicated formalities: elections in several steps, drawing by lot, and so on, which manifestly had for their purpose the obviating of bribery and corruption. Most often, the president of the tribunal (mayor, bailiff, etc.) was an officer of the seigneur's. It happened, nevertheless, that the city had something to say in his choosing. It had in every case an assurance, in the oath which he must take to respect and defend its privileges.

By the beginning of the twelfth century, and in some cases even by the end of the eleventh, a few cities were already in possession of their special tribunal. In Italy, in the south of France, in several parts of Germany, its members bore the name of "consuls." In the Netherlands and in Northern France they were called *échevins,* or aldermen. In still other places they were designated as *jurés,* or jurors. In accordance with the locality, the extent of the jurisdiction they exercised also varied quite noticeably. They did not have it everywhere in its entirety. It frequently happened that the seigneur reserved to himself certain special cases. But these local differences are of little importance. The essential thing is that every city, by the very fact that it was recognized as a legal district, had its own judges. Their competency was set by the law of the city and limited to the territory in which it applied. Sometimes in place of a single body of magistrates there were several of them, each hav-

ing its own special attributes. In many cities, and
particularly in the episcopal cities where municipal institutions were the result of insurrection,
were to be seen, side by side with the aldermen over
whom the seigneur had more or less influence, a
body of jurors presiding over matters of peace and
specially competent in cases arising out of the communal statutes. But it is impossible to go into details here; it will suffice to have indicated the
general evolution, without regard to its innumerable modifications.

In its status as a commune, the city was administered by a council (*consilium, curia,* etc.). This
council sometimes coincided with the tribunal,
and the same individuals were at once both judges
and administrators for the middle class. Most
often, however, it had its own individuality. Its
members received their authority from the commune. They were its delegates, but it did not ab-
dicate entirely in their favor. Nominated for a
very short time, they could not usurp the power
that was entrusted to them. Not until later, when
the constitution of the city had been developed
and when administration had become complicated,
did they form a real assembly upon which the influence of the people made itself felt but feebly. At
the start it was quite otherwise. The original jurors, charged with watching over the public weal,

were only representatives very similar to the select-
men of New England towns, mere executors of the
collective will. The proof of this lies in the fact
that at first they lacked one of the fundamental
characteristics of every organized body—a central
authority, a president. The "burgomasters" and
the "mayors" of the communes were, in fact, of
relatively recent creation. They did not exist much
before the thirteenth century. They belong to an
era in which the character of institutions was tend-
ing to be modified, and in which the need of a
greater centralization and a more independent
power was being felt.

The council carried on the routine administration. It had charge of finances, commerce, and industry. It ordered and supervised public works,
organized the provisioning of the city, regulated
the equipment and the deportment of the communal army, founded schools for children, provided for the upkeep of almshouses for the old and
the poor. The statutes it decreed formed a genuine
body of municipal legislation of which there existed, north of the Alps, scarcely any prior to the
thirteenth century. But a close study of these statutes leads to the conviction that they merely developed and clarified an older form of government.

Nowhere, perhaps, was the spirit of innovation
and the practical judgment of the middle class

more highly manifest than in the realm of administration. The work done there seems the more
noteworthy in that it was an original creation.
Nothing in the prior state of things could have
served as a model for it, since the needs for which
it provided were new needs. This is made clear
by a comparison, for example, of the financial system of the feudal era with that which the city communes instituted. In the first, taxes were merely a
fiscal prestation, an established and perpetual obligation taking no count of the means of the tax-
payer, bearing down only on the people, and the
proceeds of which were added to the demesnial resources of the prince or seigneur who collected
them, without any part of them being directly appropriated for the public interest. The second, on
the contrary, recognized neither exceptions nor
privileges. All burghers, enjoying equally the advantages of the commune, were equally obligated
to contribute towards the expenses. The quota of
each was in proportion to his means. At the start
it was generally calculated on the basis of income.
Many cities kept consistently to this practice up
to the end of the Middle Ages. Others substituted
for it the excise—that is to say, the indirect tax
levied on articles of consumption and especially on
foodstuffs—in such a way that the rich and the
poor were taxed according to their expenditures.

But this city-excise was in no way connected with the old market-tolls. It was as flexible as the latter were strict, as variable in accordance with the circumstances or the needs of the public as the latter were immutable. But whatever might be the form they took, the proceeds of these taxes were entirely devoted to the needs of the commune. By the end of the twelfth century, a fiscal system had been developed and at this era can be discovered the first traces of municipal accounts.

The provisioning of the city and the regulating of commerce and industry testify more clearly still to the burghers' aptitude for solving the social and economic problems which their conditions of existence put up to them. They had to provide for the subsistence of a considerable population, obliged to get its food-supply from without; to protect their workmen from foreign competition; to make certain of their supply of raw materials and to insure the exporting of their manufactures. They accomplished it by a system of regulation so marvelously adapted to its purpose that it may be considered a masterpiece of its kind. The city economy was worthy of the Gothic architecture with which it was contemporary. It created with complete thoroughness—and, it may well be said, it created *ex nihilo*—a social legislation more complete than that of any other period in history, including our own. In doing away with the middlemen between buyer and seller, it assured to the burgher the benefit of a low cost of living; it ruthlessly pursued fraud, protected the worker from competition and exploitation, regulated his labor and his wage, watched over his health, provided for apprenticeship, forbade woman- and child-labor, and at the same time succeeded in keeping in its own hands the monopoly of furnishing the neighboring country with its products and in opening up distant markets for its trade.

All this would have been impossible if the civic spirit of the burghers had not been equal to the tasks that were laid upon them. It is necessary, in fact, to go back to antiquity to find as much devotion to the public good as that of which they had given proof. *Unus subveniet alteri tamquam fratri suo*—"let each help the other like a brother"— says a Flemish charter of the twelfth century, and these words were actually a reality. As early as the twelfth century the merchants were expending a good part of their profits for the benefit of their fellow citizens—building churches, founding hospitals, buying off the market-tolls. The love of gain was allied, in them, with local patriotism. Every man was proud of his city and spontaneously devoted himself to its prosperity. This was because, in reality, each individual life depended directly upon the collective life of the municipal association. The commune of the Middle Ages had, in fact, all the essential attributes which the State exercises today. It guaranteed to all its members the security of his person and of his chattels. Outside of it he was in a hostile world, surrounded by perils and exposed to every risk. In it alone did he have a shelter, and for it he felt a gratitude which bordered upon love. He was ready to devote himself to its defense, just as he was always ready to bedeck it and make it more beautiful than its neighbors. Those magnificent cathedrals which the thirteenth century saw erected would not have been conceivable without the joyous alacrity with which the burghers contributed, by gifts, to their construction. They not only were houses of God; they also glorified the city of which they were the greatest ornament and which their majestic towers advertised afar. They were for the cities of the Middle Ages what temples were for those of antiquity.

To the ardor of local patriotism corresponded its exclusivism. From the very fact that each city constituted a State, cities saw in one another only rivals or enemies. They could not rise above the sphere of their own interests. They were self-centered, and the feeling which they bore for their neighbors resembles very closely, within narrower limits, the nationalism of our day. The civic spirit which animated them was singularly egoistic. They jealously reserved to themselves the liberties they enjoyed within their walls. The peasants who dwelt round about them did not seem to them to be compatriots at all. The one thought was to exploit them profitably. With all their might they stood on guard to prevent the peasants from freeing themselves from the industrial system of which the cities had a monopoly. The task of provisioning these cities was likewise imposed upon the peasants, who were subjected to a tyrannical protectorate whenever it was possible to do so, as in Tuscany, for example, where Florence subjected to its yoke all the surrounding countryside.

We are, however, touching here upon events which were not manifest with all their consequences until the beginning of the thirteenth century. It will suffice to have briefly sketched a tendency which, in the period of origins, was hardly more than a suggestion of what was to come. Our intention has been merely to define the city of the Middle Ages after having depicted its origin. Furthermore, it has been possible to note only its principal traits. The physiognomy which has been outlined resembles those portraits obtained by superimposing photographs one on the other. The contours of it give a countenance common to all and belonging to none of them.

If we wished, in ending this too-long chapter, to sum up its essential points in one phrase, perhaps it would be possible to say that the city of the Middle Ages, as it existed in the twelfth century, was a commercial and industrial commune living in the shelter of a fortified enclosure and enjoying a law, an administration and a jurisprudence of exception which made of it a collective, privileged personality.

Chapter VIII

CITIES AND EUROPEAN CIVILIZATION

THE birth of cities marked the beginning of a new era in the internal history of Western Europe. Until then, society had recognized only two active orders: the clergy and the nobility. In taking its place beside them, the middle class rounded the social order out or, rather, gave the finishing touch thereto. Thenceforth its composition was not to change; it had all its constituent elements, and the modifications which it was to undergo in the course of centuries were, strictly speaking, nothing more than different combinations in the alloy.

Like the clergy and like the nobility, the middle class was itself a privileged order. It formed a distinct legal group and the special law it enjoyed isolated it from the mass of the rural inhabitants which continued to make up the immense majority of the population. Indeed, as has already been seen, it was obliged to preserve intact its exceptional status and to reserve to itself the benefits arising therefrom. Freedom, as the middle class conceived it, was a monopoly. Nothing was less liberal than the caste idea which was the cause of its strength until it became, at the end of the Middle Ages, a cause of weakness. Nevertheless to that middle class was reserved the mission of spreading the idea of liberty far and wide and of becoming, without having consciously desired to be, the means of the gradual enfranchisement of the rural classes. The sole fact of its existence was due, indeed, to have an immediate effect upon these latter and, little by little, to attenuate the contrast which at the start separated them from it. In vain it strove to keep them under its influence, to refuse them a share in its privileges, to exclude them from engaging in trade and industry. It had not the power to arrest an evolution of which it was the cause and which it could not suppress save by itself vanishing.

For the formation of the city groups disturbed at once the economic organization of the country districts. Production, as it was there carried on, had served until then merely to support the life of the peasant and supply the prestations due to his seigneur. Upon the suspension of commerce, nothing impelled him to ask of the soil a surplus which it would have been impossible for him to get rid of, since he no longer had outside markets to call upon. He was content to provide for his

daily bread, certain of the morrow and longing
for no amelioration of his lot, since he could not
conceive the possibility of it. The small markets
of the towns and the burgs were too insignificant
and their demand was too regular to rouse him
enough to get out of his rut and intensify his
labor. But suddenly these markets sprang into
new life. The number of buyers was multiplied,
and all at once he had the assurance of being able
to sell the produce he brought to them. It was only
natural for him to have profited from an opportunity as favorable as this. It depended on himself alone to sell, if he produced enough, and
forthwith he began to till the lands which hitherto
he had let lie fallow. His work took on a new
significance; it brought him profits, the chance
of thrift and of an existence which became more
comfortable as it became more active. The situation was still more favorable in that the surplus
revenues from the soil belonged to him in his own
right. The claims of the seigneur were fixed by
demesnial custom at an immutable rate, so that
the increase in the income from the land benefited
only the tenant.

But the seigneur himself had a chance to profit
from the new situation wherein the development
of the cities placed the country districts. He had
enormous reserves of uncultivated land, woods,

heaths, marshes and fens. Nothing could be simpler than to put them under cultivation and through them to profit from these new outlets which were becoming more and more exigent and remunerative as the towns grew in size and multiplied in number. The increase in population would furnish the necessary hands for the work of clearing and draining. It was enough to call for men; they would not fail to show up.

By the end of the eleventh century the movement was already manifest in its full force. Monasteries and local princes thenceforth were busy transforming the idle parts of their demesnes into revenue-producing land. The area of cultivated ground which, since the end of the Roman Empire, had not been increased, kept growing continually greater. Forests were cleared. The Cistercian Order, founded in 1098, followed this new path from its very origin. Instead of adopting for its lands the old demesnial organization, it intelligently adapted itself to the new order of things. It adopted the principle of farming on a big scale and, depending upon the region, gave itself over to the most remunerative form of production. In Flanders, where the needs of the towns were greater since they themselves were richer, it engaged in raising cattle. In England, it devoted itself particularly to the sale of wool, which the same cities of Flanders consumed in greater and greater quantity.

Meanwhile, on all sides, the seigneurs, both lay and ecclesiastic, were founding "new" towns. So was called a village established on virgin soil, the occupants of which received plots of land in return for an annual rental. But these new towns, the number of which continued to grow in the course of the twelfth century, were at the same time *free* towns. For in order to attract the farmers the seigneur promised them exemption from the taxes which bore down upon the serfs. In general, he reserved to himself only jurisdiction over them; he abolished in their favor the old claims which still existed in the demesnial organization. The charter of Lorris (1155) in the Gatinais, that of Beaumont in Champagne (1182), that of Priches in the Hainault (1158) present particularly interesting types of charters of the new towns, which were also to be found everywhere in neighboring countries. That of Breteuil in Normandy, which was taken over in the course of the twelfth century by a number of localities in England, Wales, and even Ireland, was of the same nature.

Thus a new type of peasant appeared, quite different from the old. The latter had serfdom as a characteristic; the former enjoyed freedom. And this freedom, the cause of which was the economic disturbance communicated by the towns to the organization of the country districts, was itself copied after that of the cities. The inhabitants of the new towns were, strictly speaking, rural burghers. They even bore, in a good number of charters, the name of *burgenses*. They received a legal constitution and a local autonomy which was manifestly borrowed from city institutions, so much so that it may be said that the latter went beyond the circumference of their walls in order to reach the country districts and acquaint them with liberty.

And this new freedom, as it progressed, was not long in making headway even in the old demesnes, whose archaic constitution could not be maintained in the midst of a reorganized social order. Either by voluntary emancipation, or by prescription or usurpation, the seigneurs permitted it to be gradually substituted for the serfdom which had so long been the normal condition of their tenants. The form of government of the people was there changed at the same time as the form of government of the land, since both were consequences of an economic situation on the way to disappear. Commerce now supplied all the necessaries which the demesnes had hitherto been obliged to obtain by their own efforts. It was no longer essential for each of them to produce all

the commodities for which it had use. It sufficed
to go get them at some nearby city. The abbeys of
the Netherlands, which had been endowed by
their benefactors with vineyards situated either in
France or on the banks of the Rhine and the
Moselle where they produced the wine needed for
their consumption, began, at about the start of
the thirteenth century, to sell these properties
which had now become useless and whose work-
ing and upkeep henceforth cost more than they
brought in.

No example better illustrates the inevitable disappearance of the old demesnial system in an era
transformed by commerce and the new city economy. Trade, which was becoming more and more
active, necessarily favored agricultural production, broke down the limits which had hitherto
bounded it, drew it towards the towns, modernized
it, and at the same time set it free. Man was therefore detached from the soil to which he had so
long been enthralled, and free labor was substituted more and more generally for serf labor. It
was only in regions remote from commercial
highways that there was still perpetuated in its
primitive rigor the old personal serfdom and
therewith the old forms of demesnial property.
Everywhere else it disappeared, the more rapidly
especially where towns were more numerous. In

Flanders, for example, it hardly existed at all after the beginning of the thirteenth century, although, to be sure, a few traces were still preserved. Up to the end of the old order there were still to be found, here and there, men bound by the law of mortemain or subject to forced labor, and lands encumbered by various seigniorial rights. But these survivals of the past were almost always simple taxes and he who paid them had, for all that, full personal liberty.

The emancipation of the rural classes was only one of the consequences provoked by the economic revival of which the towns were both the result and the instrument. It coincided with the increasing importance of liquid capital. During the demesnial era of the Middle Ages, there was no other form of wealth than that which lay in real estate. It ensured to the holder both personal liberty and social prestige. It was the guaranty of the privileged status of the clergy and the nobility. Exclusive holders of the land, they lived by the labor of their tenants whom they protected and whom they ruled. The serfdom of the masses was the necessary consequence of such a social organization. There was no alternative save to own the land and be a lord, or to till it for another and be a serf.

But with the origin of the middle class there took its place in the sun a class of men whose ex-

istence was in flagrant contradiction to this traditional order of things. The land upon which
they settled they not only did not cultivate but did
not even own. They demonstrated and made increasingly clear the possibility of living and growing rich by the sole act of selling, or producing
exchange values.

Landed capital had been everything, and now
by the side of it was made plain the power of
liquid capital. Heretofore money had been sterile.
The great lay or ecclesiastic proprietors in whose
hands was concentrated the very scant stock of
currency in circulation, by means of either the
land taxes which they levied upon their tenants
or the alms which the congregations brought to
the churches, normally had no way of making it
bear fruit. To be sure, it was often the case that
monasteries, in time of famine, would agree to
usurious loans to nobles in distress who would
offer their lands as security. But these transactions, forbidden otherwise by canonical law, were
only temporary expedients. As a general rule cash
was hoarded by its possessors and most often
changed into vessels or ornaments for the Church,
which might be melted down in case of need.
Trade, naturally, released this captive money and
restored its proper function. Thanks to this, it
became again the instrument of exchange and the

measure of values, and since the towns were the centers of trade it necessarily flowed towards them. In circulating, its power was multiplied by the number of transactions in which it served. Its use, at the same time, became more general; payments in kind gave way more and more to payments in money.

A new notion of wealth made its appearance: that of mercantile wealth, consisting no longer in land but in money or commodities of trade measurable in money. During the course of the eleventh century, true capitalists already existed in a number of cities; several examples have been cited above, to which it is unnecessary to refer again here. These city capitalists soon formed the habit of putting a part of their profits into land. The best means of consolidating their fortune and their credit was, in fact, the buying up of land. They devoted a part of their gains to the purchase of real estate, first of all in the same town where they dwelt and later in the country. But they changed themselves, especially, into money-lenders. The economic crisis provoked by the irruption of trade into the life of society had caused the ruin of, or at least trouble to, the landed proprietors who had not been able to adapt themselves to it. For in speeding up the circulation of money a natural result was the decreasing of its value and by that

very fact the raising of all prices. The period contemporary with the formation of the cities was a
period of high cost of living, as favorable to the
business men and artisans of the middle class as it
was painful to the holders of the land who did not
succeed in increasing their revenues. By the end of
the eleventh century many of them were obliged
to have recourse to the capital of the merchants in
order to keep going. In 1127 the charter of St.
Omer mentioned, as a current practice, the loans
contracted among the burghers of the town by the
knights of the neighborhood.

But more important operations were already
current at this era. There was no lack of merchants
rich enough to agree to loans of considerable
amount. About 1082 some merchants of Liège lent
money to the abbot of St. Hubert to permit him to
buy the territory of Chavigny, and a few years
later advanced to Bishop Otbert the sums necessary to acquire from Duke Godfrey, on the point
of departing for the Crusades, his château of
Bouillon. The kings themselves had recourse, in
the course of the twelfth century, to the good services of the city financiers. William Cade was the
money-lender to the King of England. In Flanders, at the beginning of the reign of Philip Augustus, Arras had become preeminently a city of

bankers. William the Breton describes it as full
of riches, avid of lucre and glutted with usurers:

Atrabatum . . . potens urbs . . . plena
Divitiis, inhians lucris et foenore gaudens.

The cities of Lombardy and, following their
example, those of Tuscany and Provence, went
much further in carrying on that commerce which
the Church vainly sought to oppose. By the beginning of the thirteenth century, Italian bankers had
already extended their operations north of the
Alps and their progress there was so rapid that a
half century later, thanks to the abundance of
their capital and the more advanced technique of
their procedure, they had everywhere taken the
place of the local lenders.

The power of liquid capital, concentrated in
the cities, not only gave them an economic ascendancy but contributed also towards making
them take part in political life. For as long as
society had known no other power than that which
derived from the possession of the land, the clergy
and the nobility alone had had a share in the government. The feudal hierarchy was made up entirely on the basis of landed property. The fief, in
reality, was only a tenure and the relations which
it created between the vassal and his liege lord
were only a particular modality of the relations

which existed between a proprietor and a tenant.
The only difference was that the services due from
the first to the second, in place of being of an economic nature, were of a military and political nature. Just as each local prince required the help
and counsel of his vassals so, being himself a
vassal of the king, was he held on his part to similar obligations. Thus only those who held land
entered into the direction of public affairs. They
entered into them, moreover, only in paying
through their own person; that is to say, using
the appropriate expression, *consilio et auxilio*—
by their counsel and help. Of a pecuniary contribution towards the needs of their sovereign there
could be no question at an epoch when capital, in
the form of real estate alone, served merely for
the maintenance of its possessors. Perhaps the
most striking character of the feudal State was
its almost absolute lack of finances. In it, money
played no rôle. The demesnial revenues of the
prince replenished only his privy purse. It was
impossible for him to increase his resources by
taxes, and his financial indigence prevented him
from taking into his service revocable and salaried
agents. Instead of functionaries, he had only
hereditary vassals, and his authority over them
was limited to the oath of fidelity they gave him.

But as soon as the economic revival enabled him to augment his revenues, and cash, thanks to it, began to flow to his coffers, he took immediate advantage of circumstances. The appearance of bailiffs, in the course of the thirteenth century, was the first symptom of the political progress which was going to make it possible for a prince to develop a true public administration and to change his suzerainty little by little into sovereignty. For the bailiff was, in every sense of the term, a functionary. With these revocable office-holders, remunerated not by grants of land but by stewardships, there was evinced a new type of government. The bailiff, indeed, had a place outside the feudal hierarchy. His nature was quite different from that of the old justices, mayors, or castellans who carried on their functions under an hereditary title. Between them and him there was the same difference that there was between the old serfholds and the new freeholds. Identical economic causes had changed simultaneously the organization of the land and the governing of the people. Just as they enabled the peasants to free themselves, and the proprietors to substitute the quit-rent for the demesnial *mansus*, so they enabled the princes, thanks to their salaried agents, to lay hold of the direct government of their territories. This political innovation, like the social innovations with which it was contemporary, implied the diffusion of ready cash and the circulation of money. This is quite clearly shown to be the case by the fact that Flanders, where commercial life and city life were developed sooner than in the other regions of the Netherlands, knew considerably in advance of these latter the institution of bailiffs.

The connections which were necessarily established between the princes and the burghers also had political consequences of the greatest import. It was necessary to take heed of those cities whose increasing wealth gave them a steadily increasing importance, and which could put on the field, in case of need, thousands of well equipped men. The feudal conservatives had at first only contempt for the presumption of the city militia. Otto of Freisingen was indignant when he saw the communes of Lombardy wearing the helmet and cuirass and permitting themselves to cope with the noble knights of Frederick Barbarossa. But the outstanding victory won by these clodhoppers at Legnano (1176) over the troops of the emperor soon demonstrated what they were capable of. In France, the kings did not neglect to have recourse to their services and to ally them to their own interests. They set themselves up as the protectors of the communes, as the guardians of their liberties, and made the cause of the Crown seem to them to be solidary with the city franchises. Philip Augustus must have garnered the fruits of such a skilful policy. The Battle of Bouvines (1214), which definitely established the sway of the monarchy in the interior of France and caused its prestige to radiate over all Europe, was due in great part to military contingents from the cities.

The influence of the cities was not less important in England at the same era, although it was manifest in a quite different way. Here, instead of supporting the monarchy, they rose against it by the side of the barons. They helped, likewise, in the creation of parliamentary government, the distant origins of which may be dated back to the Magna Charta (1215).

It was not only in England, furthermore, that the cities claimed and obtained a more or less large share in the government. Their natural tendency led them to become municipal republics. There is but little doubt but that, if they had had the power, they would have everywhere become States within the State. But they did not succeed in realizing this ideal save where the power of the State was impotent to counterbalance their efforts.

This was the case with Italy, in the twelfth century, and later, after the definite decline of the imperial power, with Germany. Everywhere else they had not succeeded in throwing off the superior authority of the princes, whether, as in Germany and France, the monarchy was too powerful to have to capitulate before them, or whether, as in the Netherlands, their particularism kept them from combining their efforts in order to attain an independence which immediately put them at grips with one another. They remained as a general rule, then, subject to the territorial government.

But this latter did not treat them as mere subjects. It had too much need of them not to have regard for their interests. Its finances rested in great part upon them, and to the extent that they augmented the power of the State and therewith its expenses, it felt more and more frequently the need of going to the pocketbooks of the burghers. It has already been stated that in the twelfth century it borrowed their money. And this money the cities did not grant without security. They well knew that they ran great risks of never being reimbursed, and they exacted new franchises in return for the sums which they consented to loan. Feudal law permitted the suzerain to exact of his vassals only certain well defined dues which were restricted to particular cases always identical in character. It was therefore impossible for him to subject them arbitrarily to a poll-tax and to extort from them supplies, however badly needed. In this

respect the charters of the cities granted them the
most solemn guaranties. It was, then, imperative
to come to terms with them. Little by little the
princes formed the habit of calling the burghers
into the councils of prelates and nobles with whom
they conferred upon their affairs. The instances of
such convocations were still rare in the twelfth
century; they multiplied in the thirteenth; and in
the fourteenth century the custom was definitely
legalized by the institution of the Estates in which
the cities obtained, after the clergy and the nobility, a place which soon became, although the
third in dignity, the first in importance.

Although the middle classes, as we have just
seen, had an influence of very vast import upon
the social, economic and political changes which
were manifest in Western Europe in the course
of the twelfth century, it does not seem at first
glance that they played much of a rôle in the intellectual movement. It was not, in fact, until the
fourteenth century that a literature and an art was
brought forth from the bosom of the middle
classes, animated with their spirit. Until then,
learning remained the exclusive monopoly of the
clergy and employed no other tongue than the
Latin. What literature was written in the vernacu-
lar had to do solely with the nobility, or at least
expressed only the ideas and the sentiments which

pertained to the nobility as a class. Architecture and sculpture produced their masterpieces only in the construction and ornamentation of the churches. The markets and belfries, of which the oldest specimens date back to the beginning of the thirteenth century—as for example the admirable Cloth Hall of Ypres, destroyed during the Great War—remained still faithful to the architectural style of the great religious edifices.

Upon closer inspection, however, it does not take long to discover that city life really did make its own contribution to the moral capital of the Middle Ages. To be sure, its intellectual culture was dominated by practical considerations which, before the period of the Renaissance, kept it from putting forth any independent effort. But from the very first it showed that characteristic of being an exclusively lay culture. By the middle of the twelfth century the municipal councils were busy founding schools for the children of the burghers, which were the first lay schools since the end of antiquity. By means of them, instruction ceased to be furnished exclusively for the benefit of the novices of the monasteries and the future parish priests. Knowledge of reading and writing, being indispensable to the practice of commerce, ceased to be reserved for the members of the clergy alone. The burgher was initiated into them long before the noble, because what was for the noble only an intellectual luxury was for him a daily need. Naturally, the Church immediately claimed supervision over the municipal schools, which gave rise to a number of conflicts between it and the city authorities. The question of religion was naturally completely foreign to these debates. They had no other cause than the desire of the cities to control the schools created by them and the direction of which they themselves intended to keep.

However, the teaching in these communal schools was limited, until the period of the Renaissance, to elementary instruction. All who wished to have more were obliged to turn to the clerical establishments. It was from these latter that came the "clerks" who, starting at the end of the twelfth century, were charged with the correspondence and the accounts of the city, as well as the publication of the manifold Acts necessitated by commercial life. All these "clerks" were, furthermore, laymen, the cities having never taken into their service, in contradistinction to the princes, members of the clergy who by virtue of the privileges they enjoyed would have escaped their jurisdiction.

The language which the municipal scribes employed was naturally, at first, Latin. But after the first years of the thirteenth century they adopted more and more generally the use of national idioms. It was by the cities that the vulgar tongue was introduced for the first time into administrative usage. Thereby they showed an initiative which corresponded perfectly to that lay spirit of which they were the preeminent representatives in the civilization of the Middle Ages.

This lay spirit, moreover, was allied with the most intense religious fervor. If the burghers were very frequently in conflict with the ecclesiastic authorities, if the bishops thundered fulsomely against them with sentences of excommunication, and if, by way of counterattack, they sometimes gave way to decidedly pronounced anti-clerical tendencies, they were, for all of that, none the less animated by a profound and ardent faith. For proof of this is needed only the innumerable religious foundations with which the cities abounded, the pious and charitable confraternities which were so numerous there. Their piety showed itself with a naïveté, a sincerity and a fearlessness which easily led it beyond the bounds of strict orthodoxy. At all times, they were distinguished above everything else by the exuberance of their mysticism. It was this which, in the eleventh century, led them to side passionately with the religious reformers who were fighting simony and the marriage of priests; which, in the twelfth century, spread the contemplative asceticism of the Beguines and the Beghards; which, in the thirteenth century, explained the enthusiastic reception which the Franciscans and the Dominicans received. But it was this also which assured the success of all the novelties, all the exaggerations and all the deformations of religious thought. After the twelfth century no heresy cropped out which did not immediately find some followers. It is enough to recall here the rapidity and the energy with which the sect of the Albigenses spread.

Both lay and mystic at the same time, the burghers of the Middle Ages were thus singularly well prepared for the rôle which they were to play in the two great future movements of ideas: the Renaissance, the child of the lay mind, and the Reformation, towards which religious mysticism was leading.

BIBLIOGRAPHY

ASHLEY, W. J., "The Beginnings of Town Life
in the Middle Ages," *Quarterly Journal of
Economics*, Vol. X, 1896

BALLARD, A., *The English Borough in the Twelfth
Century*
Cambridge, 1914

BATERON, M., "The Laws of Breteuil," *English
Historical Review*, Vol. XV, 1900

BELOW, G. v., "Zur Entstehung der deutschen
Stadtverfassung," *Historische Zeitschrift*,
Vols. LVIII-LIX
Die Entstehung der deutschen Stadtgemeinde
Düsseldorf, 1889
Der Ursprung der deutschen Stadtverfassung
Düsseldorf, 1892

BLANCHET, A., *Les enceintes romaines de la Gaule*
Paris, 1907

BLOMMAERT, W., *Les châtelains de Flandre*
Ghent, 1915

BONVALOT, E., *Le tiers-état d'après la charte de
Beaumont et ses filiales*
Paris, 1884

DES MAREZ, G., *Étude sur la propriété foncière dans les villes du Moyen-âge et spécialement en Flandre*
Ghent, 1898

DOREN, A. J., *Untersuchungen zur Geschichte der Kaufmannsgilden des Mittelalters*
Leipzig, 1893

ESPINAS, G., *La vie urbaine de Douai au Moyen-âge*
4 vols., Paris, 1913

FLACH, J., *Les origines de l'ancienne France*, Vol. II
Paris, 1893

GÉNESTAL, R., *La tenure en bourgage*
Paris, 1900

GERLACH, W., *Die Entstehungszeit der Stadtbefestigungen in Deutschland*
Leipzig, 1913

GIRY, A., *Histoire de la ville de Saint-Omer et de ses institutions jusqu'au XIVe siècle*
Paris, 1877
Les établissements de Rouen
2 vols., Paris, 1883-1885

GROSS, C., *The Gild Merchant*
2 vols., Oxford, 1890

HEGEL, K., *Die Entstehung des deutschen Städtewesens*
Leipzig, 1898
Städte und Gilden der germanischen Völker im Mittelalter
2 vols., Leipzig, 1891

HEMMEON, M. DEW., "Burgage Tenure in Medieval England," *Harvard Historical Studies,* Vol. XX, 1914

HUVELIN, P., *Essai historique sur le droit des marchés et des foires*
Paris, 1897

KEUTGEN, F., *Untersuchungen über den Ursprung der deutschen Stadtverfassung*
Leipzig, 1895

LABANDE, H. L., *Histoire de Beauvais et de ses institutions communales*
Paris, 1892

LUCHAIRE, A., *Les communes françaises à l'époque des Capétiens directs,* new edition, with introduction by L. Halphen
Paris, 1911

MAITLAND, F. W., *Township and Borough*
Cambridge, 1898

OTTOKAR, N., *Opiti po istorii franzoukish gorodov*
Perm, 1919

PETIT-DUTAILLIS, C. E., *L'origine des villes en Angleterre,* Vol. I of the French translation of Stubbs' *Constitutional History*

PIRENNE, H., "L'origine des constitutions urbaines au Moyen-âge," *Revue historique,* Vols. LIII, LVII, 1893, 1895
"Villes, marchés et marchands au Moyen-

âge," *Revue historique*, Vol. LXVII, 1898

"La hanse flamande de Londres," *Bulletin de l'Academie de Belgique*, Classe des lettres, 1899

"Les villes flamandes avant le XIIᵉ siècle," *Annales de l'Est et du Nord*, Vol. I, 1905

Belgian Democracy—Its Early History
Manchester, 1915

PROU, M., *Les coutumes de Lorris*
Paris, 1884

RIETSCHEL, S., *Markt und Stadt in ihrem rechtlichen Verhältniss*
Leipzig, 1897
Das Burggrafenamt
Leipzig, 1905
Die civitas auf deutschem Boden
Leipzig, 1894

ROUND, J. H., "The Castles of the Norman Conquest," *Archaeologia*, Vol. LVIII, 1903

SOHM, R., *Die Entstehung des deutschen Städtewesens*
Leipzig, 1890

VANDERKINDERE, L., "La première phase de l'évolution constitutionelle des villes flamandes," *Annales de l'Est et du Nord*, Vol. I, 1905

"La notion juridique de la commune," *Bulletin de l'Academie de Belgique*, Classe des lettres, 1906

VANDER LINDEN, H., *Les gildes marchandes dans les Pays-Bas au Moyen-âge*
Ghent, 1896

WAUTERS, A., *De l'origine des premiers développements des libertés communales en Belgique*
Brussels, 1869

The numerous monographs devoted, in each country, to the particular history of a city must of course also be consulted. A list of them can be found in the national bibliographies and especially, for England, in the *Bibliography of British Municipal History* of Charles Gross.

On the other hand, it is useless to mention, despite the importance which they had in their own times, a number of works which have become antiquated today. The chief characteristics of the most important among them will be found in H. Pirenne, "L'origine des constitutions urbaines au Moyen-âge," *Revue historique*, Vol. LIII, 1893. For England, see J. Tait, "The Study of Early Municipal History in England," *Proceedings of the British Academy*, Vol. X, 1922.

As to information on the sources of city law, it will suffice to mention here:

BALLARD, A., *British Borough Charters, 1042-1216*
Cambridge, 1913

GAUPP, E. T., *Deutsche Stadtrechte des Mittelalters*
2 vols., Breslau, 1851

GENGLER, H. G., *Deutsche Stadtrechte des Mittel-
alters*
Erlangen, 1852-1866
*Codex juris municipalis Germaniae medii
aevi*
Erlangen, 1863

GIRY, A., *Documents sur les relations de la royau-
té avec les villes en France de 1180 à 1314*
Paris, 1885

KEUTGEN, F., *Urkunden zur städtischen Verfassungsgeschichte*
Berlin, 1901

INDEX

INDEX